S0-AIT-014

DICKENS, DROOD,
and the
DETECTIVES

DICKENS, DROOD, and the DETECTIVES

Ray Dubberke

VANTAGE PRESS
New York

FIRST EDITION

Published by Vantage Press, Inc.
516 West 34th Street, New York, New York 10001

Manufactured in the United States of America
ISBN: 0-533-09639-1

Library of Congress Catalog Card No.: 91-92013

0 9 8 7 6 5 4 3 2 1

To Jack Brooks

How it would have been concluded, therefore, is not mere idle speculation, or a detective-game, but an essential preliminary to any proper critical understanding.[1]

—K. J. Fielding on
The Mystery of Edwin Drood

Contents

Illustrations

Acknowledgment

My thanks to the staff of the San Francisco Public Library, and especially to those who operate the Interlibrary Loan Service, for their help in providing the materials on which this book is based.

DICKENS, DROOD, and the DETECTIVES

Chapter I

Datchery's Physique

Charles Dickens's unfinished masterpiece, *The Mystery of Edwin Drood,* poses two preliminary questions for all those who hope to penetrate its many secrets: First, did John Jasper murder his nephew Edwin Drood? And second, who is Dick Datchery, the mysterious white-haired stranger who arrives in Cloisterham some six months after Edwin's disappearance? As others have pointed out, a correct answer to the second question could well prove to be the key to *The Mystery;* successfully identifying the elusive Datchery might at last unlock the doors of the *Drood* labyrinth, and lead us to Dickens's plans for the unwritten half of his final novel.

Without further preface, let's plunge right into the search for Datchery's identity. By citing innumerable passages from *Edwin Drood* and from the author's other works, I intend to show that Dickens, looking for a detective to solve his *Mystery,* found Datchery's prototype in the pages of one of his own books. Chapter rather than page references have been provided so that anyone who wishes to check my citations can use any edition already at hand; for *Drood* itself I follow the standard twenty-three chapter arrangement.

We'll start with Dick Datchery's description in Chapter 18 of *Edwin Drood,* where he is depicted as "a white-haired personage, with black eyebrows. Being buttoned up in a tightish blue surtout, with a buff waistcoat and grey trousers, he had something of a military air. . . . This gentleman's white head was unusually large, and his shock of white hair was unusually thick and ample."

The most suggestive phrase in this brief portrait calls attention to Datchery's "tightish blue surtout." Why, one wonders, is his surtout tight? The answer most likely to be correct is the simplest: the surtout is tight because Datchery is *overweight.* That is, Dick has a large (portly, stout) body to match his unusually large head.

Because Dickens provides no other detailed descriptions of the character, there is only one item of evidence elsewhere in the text that supports this conjecture. In Chapter 23, during a conversation with the Princess Puffer, Datchery stoops down to pick up some money and "reddens with the exertion." What causes him to redden? Although he drops the coins in surprise when the Princess mentions Edwin's name, someone of Datchery's exceptional poise and self-confidence would not be likely to compound his mistake by blushing. On the contrary, what we know of his character supports a literal reading of the passage: Dick reddens because bending over *is* an exertion for a man of his age and build.

Since these few lines exhaust the evidence in *Drood* itself, we must now turn to external evidence. As a general rule, in Dickens's other novels *a large head betokens a large man.* Following is a gallery of the writer's large-headed, heavy-set males.

Pickwick Papers, Chapter 43: "Mr. Solomon Pell . . . was a fat flabby man . . . His forehead was narrow, his face wide, his head large, and his nose all on one side . . ."

Oliver Twist, Chapter 14: "a stout old gentleman, . . . Mr. Grimwig's head was such a particularly large one. . . ."

Nicholas Nickleby, Chapter 21: Scaley has "a broad round face and a large head. . . . " Chapter 22: Just as Datchery's figure is consistent with his large head, so "the face of

Mr. Crummles was quite proportionate in size to his body." Chapter 35: Tim Linkinwater is a "fat, elderly, large-faced clerk."

Barnaby Rudge, Chapter 1: John Willet is a "burly, large-headed man with a fat face. . . ."

Martin Chuzzlewit, Chapter 16: Major Pawkins is "a large gentleman . . . distinguished by a very large skull, and a great mass of yellow forehead. . . ." Later Pawkins is called the "great square Major."

Dombey and Son, Chapter 2: Mr. Chick "was a stout bald gentleman, with a very large face, and his hands continually in his pockets. . . ." Chapters 20 and 21: Major Bagstock has a body like a barrel and a "great head wagging from side to side." Chapter 23: Captain Bunsby, "who was bulky and strong," has a head like a "human, and very large" bulkhead.

David Copperfield, Chapter 11: Mr. Micawber is "a stoutish, middle-aged person, in a brown surtout and black tights and shoes, with no more hair upon his head (which was a large one and very shining) than there is upon an egg, and with a very extensive face. . . ."

Bleak House, Chapter 9: Lawrence Boythorn has a "stalwart chest . . . hands like a clean blacksmith's" and "a massive grey head" on a "figure that might have become corpulent but . . . that he gave it no rest."

Hard Times, Part 1, Chapter 4: Josiah Bounderby is "A big, loud man . . . with a great puffed head and forehead. . . ."

Little Dorrit, Part 1, Chapter 13: Casby has an "elephantine build," and a "shining bald head, which looked so very large because it shone so much." Part 1, Chapter 21: Merdle has a "broad . . . head." Part 2, Chapter 9: Casby again, "shaking his big head with the utmost benevolence." Compare the following from Part 2, Chapter 12, to the description of Datchery above: "All buttoned-up men are weighty." Part

2, Chapter 24: Sparkler is called "the Young Man-Mountain." Later in the same chapter Sparkler's head is "so very bulky and heavy."

Great Expectations, Chapter 11: A stranger (identified later as Mr. Jaggers) is described as a "burly man . . . with an exceedingly large head and a corresponding large hand." In Chapter 18, Pip notes Jaggers's "large head, his dark complexion, his deep-set eyes, his bushy black eyebrows. . . ."

Admittedly, there are some exceptions to the rule: seven characters who have large heads without being stout. Three are dwarfs: Daniel Quilp in *The Old Curiosity Shop* (Chapter 3), Phil Squod in *Bleak House* (Chapter 21), and Miss Mowcher in *David Copperfield* (Chapter 22). Three more are gawky young men: Job Trotter in *The Pickwick Papers* (Chapter 16), Noah Claypole in *Oliver Twist* (Chapter 5), and Toots in *Dombey and Son* (Chapter 11). What these three will look like when they're middle-aged like Datchery we don't know—except in the case of Toots, who immediately after his marriage to Susan Nipper grows "extremely stout" (*Dombey,* Chapter 60).

The seventh and most interesting exception is Harold Skimpole in *Bleak House* (Chapter 6), who has a large head even though he is "of a more slender figure than Mr. Jarndyce." But Skimpole's head is large for a special reason: he is a "child," Dickens tells us over and over again; and so, just like a real child, he is given a head large in proportion to the size of his body.

Adding up the members of our large-headed coterie yields a total of 24 characters, of whom 17 (or 18, if we include Toots) are mature men of heavy build. Usually only one or two appear in each book, indicating that Dickens, by not bestowing this feature too liberally, meant to keep it distinctive. In any case, it is apparent that the author endowed certain specific character types with large heads. As for Dick

Datchery, he is not a dwarf, or a gangly youth, or a "child" like Skimpole. Instead he is another in Dickens's long line of stout, middle-aged men with large, imposing heads, like Mr. Jaggers and Wilkins Micawber.

Another thought-provoking (and much-discussed) question about Datchery's appearance is whether the "shock of white hair" is his own or a wig, but because the answer makes little difference to my theory of his identity, I prefer at present not to waste time on this white herring.

Chapter II

Latecomers

I believe that Dick Datchery is his own man, a new character who makes his debut in Chapter 18 of *Edwin Drood.* The majority of commentators, however, have asserted that Datchery is one of the novel's other characters in disguise. In support of their position, many of these critics claim that the introduction of an important new character late in a novel is contrary to Dickens's usual methods.[1]

While it is true that Dickens introduced most major characters early in his stories, there are exceptions to the supposed rule against late introductions in twelve of his fifteen novels, stragglers who drop in when the action is well under way. For purposes of comparison, Datchery first appears in Chapter 18, on page 206 of 278 in my edition.[2] (Page numbers are given solely to demonstrate my method; the same results will obtain regardless of the edition used—but adjust as needed so that the story starts with page one.) As *Drood* was only half finished at the author's death, its total length when completed would have been somewhere in the neighborhood of 556 pages. Dividing 206 by 556, we find that Datchery arrived when Dickens had written about 37 percent of the projected total. How does Dick's arrival compare with that of other latecomers?

Edwin Drood: Tartar makes his entry just a few pages before Datchery, in Chapter 17 on page 202 (36 percent).

Our Mutual Friend: Several important characters arrive fairly late in the narrative: Bradley Headstone in Book Two, Chapter 1, page 221 of 850 (26 percent); Jenny Wren in the same chapter, page 227 (27 percent); "Fascination" Fledgeby in Book Two, Chapter 4, page 266 (31 percent); and Mr. Riah in Book Two, Chapter 5, page 283 (33 percent).

Tale of Two Cities: Gabelle the Postmaster, who motivates Darnay's return to Paris, is first mentioned in Chapter 8 of Book II, page 108 of 370 (29 percent).

Hard Times: James Harthouse, Louisa's would-be seducer, enters in the seventeenth chapter of 37, page 106 of 268 (40 percent).

Bleak House: Inspector Bucket is introduced in Chapter 22 of 67, page 318 of 911 (35 percent). Keep this in mind, as I'll have much more to say about Mr. Bucket later.

David Copperfield: Uriah Heep, Mr. Wickfield, and Agnes Wickfield all turn up in Chapter 15 of 64, pages 208–212 of 837 (25 percent). More significantly, Dora Spenlow, David's child-bride, is not presented until Chapter 26, page 366 (44 percent).

Dombey and Son: Edith Granger, Mr. Dombey's second wife, makes his acquaintance (and ours) in Chapter 21 of 62, page 274 of 839 (33 percent). Several minor characters of some importance to the plot—Harriet Carker, Cousin Feenix, and Alice Marwood—appear even later.

Martin Chuzzlewit: Mrs. Sairey Gamp appears in Chapter 19 of 54, page 273 of 734 (37 percent). The secret inquiry agent Nadgett, who pursues Jonas Chuzzlewit in much the same way that Datchery does Jasper, enters in Chapter 27, page 393 (54 percent).

Barnaby Rudge: Lord George Gordon, secretary Gashford, and servant John Grueby are all introduced in Chapter 35 of 82, page 237 of 574 (41 percent). Dennis the Hangman comes to our notice in Chapter 36, page 246 (43 percent).

Old Curiosity Shop: The "single gentleman" (Little Nell's granduncle) and Dick Swiveller's "Marchioness" both show up in Chapter 34 of 73, page 249 of 541 (46 percent).

Oliver Twist: "Monks"—Oliver's villainous half-brother, Edward Leeford—is first mentioned in Chapter 26 of 53, page 207 of 457 (45 percent). The Bow Street officers Blathers and Duff, lesser characters but detectives like Bucket and Nadgett, appear on the scene in Chapter 31, page 245 (54 percent).

Pickwick Papers: While the characters who come late in *Pickwick* are relatively minor, they bring with them what little plot there is: Dodson and Fogg in Chapter 18 of 57, page 250 of 817 (31 percent); Arabella Allen in Chapter 28, page 388 (47 percent); and Ben Allen and Bob Sawyer in Chapter 30, page 415 (51 percent).

As these facts demonstrate, Dickens regularly introduced significant characters after the quarter point in his novels, and he presented Datchery no later than most. While the evidence demolishes the argument that Dick is likely to be someone else in disguise merely because he arrives late, it does not in itself prove that he is a new character. To settle that point, it is necessary to show that none of the "old" characters sufficiently resembles him to assume convincingly the role of the white-haired stranger.

Chapter III

Rejects

To overlook no one, we are obliged to consider no less than seven characters for the part of Dick Datchery: Edwin Drood, Neville and Helena Landless, Hiram Grewgious, Luke Honeythunder, Lieutenant Tartar, and Bazzard the law clerk. How well does each of them qualify?

Edwin Drood since boyhood has been on close terms with his uncle John Jasper, who in turn ought to recognize his nephew Ned under a wig, however thick and ample. Moreover, Drood knows Cloisterham well; there is no reason for him to lose his way (as Datchery does in Chapter 18) in seeking the Tope residence. Dickens emphasizes Edwin's youthfulness by describing him in Chapter 2 as "the boy (for he is little more)"; and Edwin in Chapter 3 says of himself, "I am not clever out of my own line." Yet if Drood is Datchery, this not-too-clever boy is capable of playing a very clever middle-aged man so expertly that he can fool his own uncle.

The same objections apply to Neville and Helena Landless: they are too young, they know Cloisterham, and Jasper knows them. They have the additional disadvantages of being slender and supple (Chapter 6) while Datchery is stout, and of being "both very dark, and very rich in colour." Sapsea finds Neville's complexion "un-English" (Chapter 14) but mentions no such flaw in Dick Datchery. Finally, Dickens applies to the twins such adjectives as "untamed," "half shy, half defiant," "fierce of look," and (to Helena alone) "gipsy type," none of which even remotely fits Datchery.

Hiram Grewgious too is known to Jasper, and he has no trouble in finding his way from Miss Twinkleton's school to the gatehouse and the Cathedral in Chapter 9. In the drawings by Luke Fildes, made under Dickens's close supervision, Grewgious is a thin, "Angular" man, not a stout, large-headed personage like Datchery. Furthermore, Dickens says of the lawyer in Chapter 11, "The apprehension of dying suddenly, and leaving one fact or figure with any incompleteness or obscurity attaching to it, would have stretched Mr. Grewgious stone-dead any day." It is hard to reconcile this meticulous character with someone like Datchery, who records his observations by making irregular chalkmarks on a cupboard door; and almost impossible to imagine the glib Mr. Datchery doting on the woman he loved, as Grewgious did, "at a hopeless, speechless distance" (Chapter 11).

Surprisingly, no one has proposed Luke Honeythunder for the part of Datchery, even though he meets the physical requirements of the role: he is a large man (Chapter 6) and presumably of middle age. In addition, as Neville's guardian he has a motive for coming to the young man's assistance. However, Honeythunder has been to Cloisterham at least once, when he attended the Crisparkles' dinner party, and on that occasion Jasper met him and accordingly should recognize the philanthropist's "strongly marked face" if Honeythunder later reappears as Datchery. Besides, this "Boil upon the face of society," who never sees a joke, surely cannot transform himself into the suave and accommodating stranger.

Lieutenant Tartar, on the other hand, has the right personality, is unknown to Jasper, and does not know Cloisterham. But at "eight-and-twenty, or at the utmost thirty" (Chapter 17) he is too young to be the idle buffer, and his physical condition is too good. Tartar and Lobley pulling a pair of oars (in Chapter 22) "seemed to take it easily, . . . yet their oars bent as they pulled, and the boat bounded under them. Mr. Tartar talked as if he were doing nothing. . . ." In the very next chapter, this same man—if Tartar is Datchery—"reddens with the exertion" of stooping over to pick up a few coins. Also, why would someone "bred in the Royal Navy" since adolescence (Chapter 17), who accordingly knows little else, confess himself to be a retired diplomat rather than a retired naval officer (Chapter 18)?

Grewgious's clerk Bazzard is the candidate nominated most frequently to be Datchery. This too is surprising, since this "particularly Angular clerk" (Chapter 9) with his "dissatisfied doughy complexion" and "gloomy" manner (Chapter 11) seems to be totally unlike the cheerful Datchery. What misleads Bazzard's advocates is Grewgious's remark in Chapter 20 that his clerk "is off duty here, altogether, just at present." Obviously Bazzard is on some sort of special assignment, but is it his mission to go to Cloisterham in the guise of Datchery, or does he have another task more suited to his position and personality?

To Hiram Grewgious, there are three conceivable explanations for the disappearance of Edwin Drood: (1) He absconded for some reason and is still alive; or (2) He was murdered by John Jasper; or (3) He was murdered by Neville Landless. While Grewgious suspects Jasper (Chapter 15), he is a fair-minded, cautious man not given to jumping to conclusions; thus we can expect him to investigate equally all three possibilities. As he says in Chapter 21, "It is a business principle of mine, in such a case, not to close up any direction, but to keep an eye on every direction that may present itself. I could relate an anecdote in point, but that it would be premature."

How does Grewgious probe the three directions in the Drood case? As to the first, the lawyer's main recourse in this direction is simply to wait for Edwin's birthday. If Drood is alive, he will almost certainly report to his father's engineering firm to claim his inheritance when he comes of age in May. (See the conversation between Grewgious and Jasper in Chapter 9 pertaining to Edwin's future.) By the end of Chapter 17, "Full half a year had come and gone" since Edwin's disappearance; Neville and Helena have come of age, and the termination of Honeythunder's guardianship accentuates this fact; Drood too has attained his majority but he has not returned to claim his partnership. This being the case, Grewgious can only conclude that Edwin is dead, and so "At about this time a stranger appeared in Cloisterham"; i.e., Datchery arrived to ferret out Jasper's culpability. But what does Grewgious do about Neville Landless?

When Septimus Crisparkle calls on Mr. Grewgious in Chapter 17, we learn that it was the lawyer who recommended Neville's lodgings in Staple Inn to Crisparkle. Grewgious then says of Neville, "I entertain a sort of fancy for having him under my eye." Dickens adds, "As Mr. Grewgious had to turn his eye up considerably before he could see the chambers, the phrase was to be taken figuratively and not literally." Under whose eye was Neville literally at this moment? Not Tartar's—when Grewgious entertained this particular fancy he had yet to meet the lieutenant.

Note that Bazzard is not present during Crisparkle's visit to the lawyer's office. From his employer's remarks I infer that it is Bazzard who has his eye on young Landless, and that this watch upon Neville is the clerk's special assignment. Later, when John Jasper comes to London to hound Neville, Bazzard's surveillance at Staple Inn expands to include "our local friend" as well.

But Bazzard has an even more important contribution to make. To entice the choirmaster to return to the place where he concealed his nephew's body, someone has to tell Jasper about the ring that Grewgious entrusted to Drood in Chapter 11. Only three people in the novel are aware of the existence and the significance of this ring: Grewgious, Drood, and Bazzard. Grewgious can't tell because his doing so would arouse Jasper's suspicions; Drood can't tell because he "has long been given up, as dead"; thus Bazzard must be the one who reveals the secret to Jasper.

Nor would this revelation be difficult to arrange. With Jasper shadowing Neville, and Bazzard keeping watch on both of them, the two surveillants are bound to meet. When they do, Bazzard will tell Jasper how Grewgious gave the ring to Drood. This development explains the dichotomy in Bazzard's character: Dickens made him disagreeable and dissatisfied so that the unwary reader would accept his pretended betrayal of his employer; but the clerk will justify Grewgious's high opinion of him when his "treachery" is later revealed as the first step in the plan to trap the murderer.

To sum up, Bazzard is not Datchery because his personality is all wrong for the role and because the part he is to play in the eventual denouement precludes his becoming known to Jasper as an old buffer in Cloisterham. Nor does any other character in *Edwin Drood* bear more than a superficial resemblance to the mysterious stranger. But is there anyone elsewhere whom Datchery does closely resemble?

Chapter IV

Bucket and Datchery

In all of Charles Dickens's writings, the character who most resembles Dick Datchery, both in appearance and behavior, is Inspector Bucket of *Bleak House.* Like Bucket, Datchery is a latecomer who appears only after most of the other characters have been introduced;[1] again like Bucket, when he does enter, Datchery exerts a strong influence on the development of the story.

Here is Bucket as himself (*BH,* Chapter 22): "He is a stoutly-built, steady-looking, sharp-eyed man in black, of about the middle age." And here's Bucket in a grey wig, disguised as an elderly doctor (*BH,* Chapter 24): "a very respectable old gentleman, with grey hair, wearing spectacles, and dressed in a black spencer and gaiters and a broad-brimmed hat. . . ." Put these two passages together, remove the false spectacles, and change to suitable clothes, and this is the result: a stoutly-built, steady-looking, sharp-eyed man, of late middle age; a very respectable gentleman, with grey hair, and dressed in a tightish blue surtout, buff waistcoat, and grey trousers. Voilà! The character has become a dead ringer for Dick Datchery!

But Datchery resembles Bucket in more than appearance. Bucket throughout the course of *Bleak House* conducts himself with affable self-assurance, in exactly the same manner as Datchery in the completed chapters of *Edwin Drood.*

Both are obviously men who know what they're doing and enjoy doing it. What's more, many of Bucket's personal traits and mannerisms turn up again in Datchery, as the following paragraphs will show.

Prowling about the streets of London, Bucket "seems in some undefinable manner to lurk and lounge" (*BH,* Chapter 22) ". . . to outward appearance rather languishing for want of an object" (*BH,* Chapter 53). On the streets of Cloisterham, Datchery "lounges along, like the chartered bore of the city, with his uncovered grey hair blowing about" (*ED,* Chapter 23).

Bucket catches Lady Dedlock's attention when he "rattles something in his pocket—halfpence perhaps" (*BH,* Chapter 53), and Datchery attracts the Opium Woman's greedy ears by "rattling the loose money in the pockets of his trousers" (*ED,* Chapter 23).

Pumping Jo for information, "Bucket stealthily tells the coins from one hand to the other like counters—which is a way he has, his principal use of them being in these games of skill" (*BH,* Chapter 22). Playing the same game with the Princess Puffer, Datchery "begins very slowly to count out the sum demanded of him . . . stops in his counting, finds he has counted wrong, shakes his money together, and begins again . . . pauses with the selected coins in his hand, rather as if he . . . couldn't bear to part with them" (*ED,* Chapter 23).

Invariably addressing the self-important Dedlock as "Sir Leicester Dedlock, Baronet," Bucket "delights in a full title, and does violence to himself when he dispenses with any fragment of it" (*BH,* Chapter 54). Speaking to the pompous Mr. Sapsea in the third person as "The Worshipful the Mayor" or "His Honour the Mayor," Datchery similarly employs "a great, not to say a grand, address, accustomed to rank and dignity" (*ED,* Chapter 18).

Bucket displays "adaptability to all grades" of society (*BH,* Chapter 53), and Datchery obviously does likewise in gaining the confidence of Deputy, Mr. and Mrs. Tope, Sapsea, Durdles, and the Princess Puffer (*ED,* Chapters 18 and 23).

Bucket's father was an innkeeper (*BH,* Chapter 53), and Datchery likes "the old tavern way of keeping scores" (*ED,* Chapter 23).

The inspector manifests "a certain enjoyment of the work" in which he's engaged (*BH,* Chapter 57), while the buffer reveals his enjoyment of the work when he chalks up his score on the cupboard door (*ED,* Chapter 23).

Bucket is employed on private business by the old lawyer Tulkinghorn (*BH,* Chapter 22), and Datchery almost certainly is sent to Cloisterham by the old lawyer Grewgious.

Now for the clincher. "Mr. Bucket makes a leg," a kind of male curtsey, in greeting Lady Dedlock (*BH,* Chapter 53). Mr. Datchery makes a leg when he meets Jasper and Sapsea (*ED,* Chapter 18). *These are the only occurrences of this gesture in all of Dickens's novels.*[2]

There is a point beyond which an accumulation of facts rules out the possibility of coincidence. All these similarities between Inspector Bucket and Dick Datchery are not fortuitous, nor was Dickens unaware of them. Rather he purposely introduced them to convey subtly the impression that Datchery, like Bucket before him, is a Scotland Yard detective. But can we go a step further? If Datchery resembles Bucket in so many ways, are the two one and the same person—is Datchery actually Inspector Bucket in another disguise? My answer is no, for three reasons.

First, Dickens carried characters over from a previous book only once, in *Master Humphrey's Clock,* and the reintroduction there of Mr. Pickwick and the Wellers was a disappointment. It is not likely that his last novel would repeat this experiment, especially since some sixteen years had elapsed between the publication of *Bleak House* (1853) and the inception of *Edwin Drood* (1869).

Second, Bucket's most striking characteristic is his remarkable fat forefinger. Nowhere in *Drood* is Datchery's forefinger mentioned. While Dickens would have had to suppress such a dead giveaway, without his forefinger Bucket just wouldn't be Bucket.

Third, and most conclusive, except in his disguise as the old physician Bucket speaks working-class English, while Dick Datchery consistently uses middle-class English, even in soliloquy. If he were Bucket, Datchery would revert to his natural manner of speech when talking to himself.

No, Datchery is not Bucket. But then, who is he?

Detail from *Reading the Will*
Painted by Sir David Wilkie, Engraved by William Greatbach

Chapter V

Datchery Discovered

As most Dickensians know, the character of Inspector Bucket was based on a real-life Scotland Yard detective named Charles Frederick Field, whom Dickens met, along with a group of other detective police officers, shortly before he wrote *Bleak House.* Accounts of his meetings with these detectives appeared in several articles in Dickens's magazine *Household Words,* and are available in the book *Reprinted Pieces.*

While Inspector Field was unquestionably the officer who made the most marked impression on Dickens, the author—in his article "The Detective Police"—enthusiastically expressed his admiration for the entire group: "They are, one and all, respectable-looking men; of perfectly good deportment and unusual intelligence; with nothing lounging or slinking in their manners; with an air of keen observation and quick perception when addressed; and generally presenting in their faces, traces more or less marked of habitually leading lives of strong mental excitement."

Like Field, another detective makes several appearances in the articles. This was Sergeant Stephen Thornton, renamed Dornton by Dickens in *Household Words.* In "The Detective

Police" the author gives us this description of Thornton/ Dornton:

> Sergeant Dornton about fifty years of age, with a ruddy face and a high sunburnt forehead, has the air of one who has been a Sergeant in the Army—he might have sat to Wilkie for the Soldier in the Reading of the Will. He is famous for steadily pursuing the inductive process, and, from small beginnings, working on from clue to clue until he bags his man.

As you have already guessed, "Dornton" is my candidate for the original from whom Dick Datchery was derived. He is the right age; he has Datchery's military air; and his English, unlike that of his brother officers, is middle-class. In "The Adventures of a Carpet Bag" he displays a sense of humor akin to Datchery's; and in "The Sofa" a degree of compassion perhaps rare in members of his profession, when he tells the young man whom he has just arrested for theft, "I regret, for the sake of yourself and your friends, that you should have done what you have; but this case is complete."

There is even a hint that "the soldierly-looking man" has a larger-than-average head. In "The Sofa" Sergeant Dornton says of himself, "My face . . . was pale at that time, my health not being good; and looked as long as a horse's." A long head might well have become a large one when Dornton recovered his health and put on some weight.

Illustrating this chapter is a detail from Sir David Wilkie's *Reading the Will.* It reproduces a print in *The Wilkie Gallery,*[1] a collection of etchings based on the artist's works, and is thus the version with which Dickens and his readers were familiar. The original painting, commissioned in 1819 by the King of Bavaria, hangs to this day in Munich, Germany, and so was inaccessible to Dickens's contemporary audience. While the relative size of the soldier's head and body is difficult to discern in either rendering, Allan Cunningham in his

Life of Sir David Wilkie (1843)[2] described the young widow's admirer as "a brawny officer"—surely an adjective Dickens might have bestowed on one of his weighty men.

Remember Datchery's shock of white hair? Sergeant Dornton's "high forehead" leads me to believe that Datchery *is* wearing a wig. There are obvious reasons for a professional detective to adopt such a disguise: it allows a successful, perhaps even famous sleuth to avoid recognition, and (by adding a few years to his age) makes possible his cover as a retired diplomat. Nevertheless, I won't insist upon the wig.[3] Since an author in his omnipotence can accomplish the otherwise miraculous, Dickens in transforming Dornton into Datchery may have decided to grow a flowing head of hair on the detective's sunburnt dome.

At this point, someone may protest that the *Household Words* articles were written some twenty years before *Edwin Drood.* How could Dickens be expected to remember Dornton so well after all those years? As it happens, he didn't have to—for the author in 1867 or 1868 carefully corrected the articles in *Reprinted Pieces* for their inclusion in his collected works. Further evidence that these articles were fresh in Dickens's mind appears in the name of Datchery's young assistant, Deputy. In the article "On Duty with Inspector Field," the inspector tells Dickens "that the man who takes care of the beds and lodgers" in these "low lodging-houses . . . for travellers" is always called Deputy. The boy Deputy repeats this explanation in *Edwin Drood* (Chapter 5): "All us man-servants at Travellers' Lodgings is named Deputy." By giving the detective's helper this name, Dickens points to his *Household Words* articles and through them to Datchery's identity.

Dick Datchery's own name also furnishes food for thought. Just as Dickens converted Thornton to Dornton, so Datchery is probably his variation on the common English surname Thatcher. To wit: Thornton, Dornton; Thatcher,

Datchery. Perhaps the name Thornton suggested the similar name Thatcher; or perhaps the name of another officer mentioned in "The Detective Police" brought the word to Dickens's mind. A thatcher is someone who thatches *straw;* and one of the detectives who met with Dickens was Sergeant Frederick Shaw—whom the writer christened "Sergeant Straw"![4]

As for the given name Dick, there are several reasons why Dickens may have chosen this particular nickname; for now I'll mention just one. For some years prior to his retirement in 1863, Stephen Thornton was one of two ranking inspectors at the Detective Department, Scotland Yard; the other was Jonathan Whicher (who appears as Sergeant Witchem in "The Detective Police"). In *The Moonstone* (1868), Dickens's friendly rival Wilkie Collins modeled his detective character Sergeant Richard Cuff upon Inspector Whicher. (Perhaps "Whicher" even inspired "Richard.") Since Collins employed Whicher, it may have amused Dickens to base his character on Thornton, and to give him the same first name!

Even the Opium Woman elicits what may be a smidgen of evidence when she asks Datchery, "Whisper. What's his name, deary?" and he replies, "Surname Jasper, Christian name John. Mr. John Jasper" (*ED,* Chapter 23). Certainly a distinctive way to state a person's name—reminiscent of an entry on a police blotter.

Of greater significance is the title of Bazzard's play, "The Thorn of Anxiety," which he and Grewgious hope will come out at last. Probably this "dreadfully appropriate name" conceals another clue: the secret of Datchery's identity can be construed as a thorn of anxiety, to Dickens as well as his readers, and this Thorn(ton) was surely meant to come out at last.

One item of negative evidence may be worth considering here. In the completed portion of the novel, there is absolutely no police involvement in the disappearance of Edwin Drood. We know there are policemen in Cloisterham, because at the beginning of Chapter 19 Dickens mentions "the Cloisterham police meanwhile looking askant from their beats with suspicion" at some dusty wayfarers. We also know that Charles Collins's preliminary sketch for the cover of the serialized novel showed three police constables on the right-hand side above the male opium smoker, but the final illustration for the cover wrapper substitutes two civilians for the three officers. Why were the policemen replaced?

If Dickens planned all along to bring in a police specialist from London, he had no need to involve the local constabulary in his mystery. And this omission is historically justifiable, because there would have been only "preventive" police but no detectives on duty in "Cloisterham" at the time the story is set. Based on internal evidence (such as the remark in Chapter 6 that "In those days there was no railway in Cloisterham"), Percy Carden has cogently postulated the date of Drood's disappearance as December 24, 1842.[5] In August *of that same year,* the Detective Department was founded at Scotland Yard. At that time the eight officers selected to staff it constituted the only publicly employed detective force in all of England, the famous Bow Street "Runners" having been disbanded in 1839 by Act of Parliament. No doubt Dickens knew that small towns like Cloisterham had no police detectives of their own in 1842; perhaps he even placed the disappearance in that year to prevent a premature investigation and to allow his detective to come from London incognito.

And just possibly Dickens was also aware that one of the eight founding members of the original Detective Department was a sergeant named Stephen Thornton—so the soldierly-looking man was available to go to Cloisterham in June 1843.[6] But he went as a brand-new character, not as Thornton or Dornton; for Stephen Thornton bears the same relationship to Dick Datchery as Charles Frederick Field does to Inspector Bucket, the real person being merely the starting point for the Dickensian persona.

Thus we have, like "Dornton" himself, worked on from clue to clue until we bagged our man. Perhaps the most satisfying aspect of my association of Dick Datchery with the eminent Scotland Yard detective Stephen Thornton is that there is nothing silly about it. To identify Datchery as Drood, Helena, Grewgious, Bazzard, or even Tartar is to make him a kind of white-wigged freak. Charles Dickens was the most popular novelist of his age for a reason—he had an uncanny instinct for pleasing his readers. I find it inconceivable that he would disappoint them in his choice of a detective hero for his last book.

Chapter VI

Relevant Crimes

With just a few exceptions, the evidence so far presented has come from Charles Dickens's own writings, but there are some substantiating data from other sources to support the hypothesis that the character called Dick Datchery was based upon Stephen Thornton of the Metropolitan Police. Such secondary evidence is necessarily more speculative than that gleaned from the author's own works, but it will help to complete the case in favor of the Scotland Yard detective.

It is a well-documented fact that Charles Dickens was a true-crime buff. As his friend and protégé George Augustus Sala once said of him, "What he liked to talk about was . . . the latest exciting trial or police case, . . . and especially the latest murder and the newest thing in ghosts. . . . Dickens had a curious and almost morbid partiality for communing with and entertaining police officers."[1] Philip Collins tells us the author was an avid follower of murder trials who "was not above visiting the scene of the crime."[2] And Dickens himself relates how, whenever he visited Paris, he was "dragged by invisible force into the Morgue."[3] Here he checked out the bodies with evident relish, wishing with his fellow onlookers that each corpse "had been killed by human agency—his own, or somebody else's: the latter preferable."[4]

John Thurtell

A chronological glance at just a few comments by and about Dickens establishes that this fascination for crime flourished throughout his life. Thus he cited John Thurtell, whose murder of William Weare in 1823 made an indelible impression on the eleven-year-old author-to-be, as "one of the murderers best remembered in England";[5] on a visit to Newgate Prison in 1837, he observed the artist-cum-murderer Thomas Griffiths Wainewright reading in a cell; he attended the hangings of François Courvoisier in 1840 and of Frederick and Maria Manning in 1849; noted in 1856 the similarities in behavior between John Thurtell and "The Poisoner," William Palmer of Rugeley;[6] praised the judge who tried and condemned to death another alleged poisoner, Thomas Smethurst, in 1859; expressed the hope, in October 1864, that the first railway murderer, Franz Müller, would be executed; and, when Oliver Wendell Holmes showed him around Harvard University in 1868, asked to see first the laboratory where Prof. John White Webster had murdered Dr. George Parkman back in 1849.

Given Dickens's lifelong interest in and knowledge of the sensational crimes of his day, it is not surprising to find that he used several incidents from actual murder cases when he wrote *The Mystery of Edwin Drood.* For example, after the Mannings murdered Patrick O'Connor, they dug a grave in their back kitchen, covered the body with quicklime, and repaved the floor over the grave—an attempt to hide and destroy the remains not dissimilar from the method used by John Jasper. As many commentators agree, the choirmaster immures his victim in Mrs. Sapsea's tomb and employs quicklime in trying to dispose of Drood's body.

An even more striking parallel can be found in the case of Constance Kent. When she was eleven years old, Constance ran away from home with her brother William, then age ten, apparently because the two children felt neglected

Professor Webster Murders Doctor Parkman

by their father and stepmother, who favored the children of Mr. Kent's second marriage over those of his first wife. Constance was the leader of this escapade, in which she displayed great initiative and resourcefulness, cutting short her hair and dressing in boys' clothing to conceal her identity. Together the children set out for Bristol, intending to go to sea. When they were stopped and questioned in Bath, William quickly broke down and confessed that his name was Kent, but Constance resolutely refused to talk, "displaying throughout an amount of nerve which amazed all beholders."[7] Compare this exploit with Neville Landless's account, in Chapter 7 of *Edwin Drood,* of the times when he and his sister Helena fled from their brutal stepfather: "When we ran away . . . (we ran away four times in six years, to be brought back and cruelly punished), the flight was always of her planning and leading. Each time she dressed as a boy, and showed the daring of a man." Clearly Helena's behavior on these occasions was based on that of Constance Kent.

Incidents from the Stepney murder case of 1860 reveal a similar resemblance to events in *Edwin Drood.* When it occurred, the case was "much discussed in legal circles and the Press,"[8] and *The Annual Register* for that year commented somewhat hyperbolically, "The Stepney murder will remain memorable in the annals of crime, for it was attended by a combination of circumstances which read more like the complicated guilt of a French novel, or an Adelphi drama, than a possible occurrence in real life."[9] I feel certain that Dickens borrowed some of the singular features of this case (an account of which follows) in constructing the plot of *Edwin Drood.*

A wealthy seventy-year-old widow named Mary Emsley was murdered in Stepney on August 14, 1860. Mrs. Emsley owned several houses, and it was rumored that she kept her tenants' rent money in her home. One of her part-time rent collectors, a cobbler named Walter Emm, became suspicious when his employer failed to come to her door in response to his knocking. He notified the police, who broke into the house and found the widow upstairs with her head battered in by a hammer-like weapon. Sir Richard Mayne, Commissioner of the Metropolitan Police, assigned Inspector Stephen Thornton to take charge of the investigation, assisted by Sergeants Thomas and Tanner.

Because the victim was known to keep her doors and windows carefully locked, because she was very suspicious of strangers, and because there were no signs of a forcible entry, Inspector Thornton suspected from the first that Mrs. Emsley had been killed by someone she knew and trusted. A witness reported seeing a plasterer and handyman named George Mullins,[10] who did repair work on the widow's property, walking along the street with bulging pockets early on the morning after the murder, and observed that Mullins seemed to be "in a state of great nervous excitement." Mullins was questioned closely by Thornton and Thomas, but he was able to convince them that he had had nothing to do with the crime. One of the points in the handyman's favor was his status as a retired police sergeant and former member of the Royal Irish Constabulary. Another was his looks: "He is described as 58 years of age, of intelligent and rather prepossessing appearance."[11]

Several weeks passed without an arrest, and the newspapers began to voice their usual complaints about the inefficiency of the police and the inactivity of the government. To allay this criticism, a reward of £300 was offered for information leading to the arrest and conviction of the murderer, but this offer at first produced no results. Then one evening George Mullins turned up at the home of Sergeant Richard Tanner, who happened to live in Mullins's neighborhood. The former policeman had an interesting story to tell. He had become suspicious of Mr. Emm, and, from the vantage point of an herb field near Emm's home, had been keeping an eye on the cobbler for several days. Early on the previous morning he had seen Emm take a package from the cottage where he lived to a shed beside it. A short while later, Emm had come out of the shed without the package. Mullins, who prided himself on his detective skills, inferred that Emm had hidden some of the loot from Mrs. Emsley's murder in the shed.

When Dick Tanner advised Mullins that Inspector Thornton would have to be informed, the ex-policeman agreed on condition that he would get the £300 reward if anything came of his information. The next morning officers Thornton, Tanner, and Thomas picked up Mullins at his home and went together to Emm's cottage. While the others waited outside, Tanner searched the cottage but found nothing incriminating, and returned to tell Thornton. "No, no!" exclaimed Mullins impatiently at this point, "It's not in the cottage! The package is hidden behind a stone slab in the shed!"

On searching the shed, the detectives soon found the stone slab and behind it a parcel tied with the type of waxed thread used by cobblers. Inside the parcel were some stolen spoons and a renter's check payable to Mrs. Emsley. The officers decided to arrest Mr. Emm, but to Mullins's surprise Thornton arrested him too. No further evidence was found against Mr. Emm, who denied all knowledge of the loot in his shed, but a thorough search of Mullins's home turned up a plasterer's hammer with the same type of head as the weapon that had smashed in Mary Emsley's skull, a discarded boot that matched a bloody footprint at the scene of the crime, a lump of cobbler's wax, and some apron string that corresponded to one of the strings around the parcel in Mr. Emm's shed. As it was obvious that Mullins had planted the evidence in the shed to get the reward money, the cobbler was soon released from custody, while George Mullins was ultimately hanged for Mrs. Emsley's murder. What had led to his downfall, of course, was the fact that, from his post in the herb field, it was impossible to see the stone slab in the shed, let alone the package behind it.

George Mullins's misstep, which spoiled an otherwise "perfect crime," must have struck Dickens as a remarkable illustration of one of his favorite maxims. According to his daughter, Kate Dickens Perugini, "He often said, that the most clever criminals were constantly detected through some small defect in their calculations. . . . [This was] the pet theory that he so frequently mentioned whenever a murder case was brought to trial."[12]

What does all this have to do with *The Mystery of Edwin Drood*? There was an old tradition in Rochester concerning a certain uncle who murdered his nephew and buried the body under a building near his home.[13] Blend the facts of the Stepney murder with those of the Rochester tradition—that is, convert handyman to uncle and widow to nephew, and hide the body—and what you get is the plot of *Edwin Drood.* To recapitulate, George Mullins murdered someone who trusted him implicitly—his employer, Mary Emsley. Because he was a retired police officer, the handyman appeared to be above suspicion. But then he overreached himself by trying to implicate an innocent man—Walter Emm. The detective in charge of the police investigation, who arrested Mullins and found the evidence to convict him, was Stephen Thornton. In Dickens's story, John Jasper also murders someone who trusts him implicitly—his nephew, Edwin Drood. Because he is the choirmaster of Cloisterham Cathedral, Jasper appears to be above suspicion. But he too overreaches himself when he tries to incriminate an innocent man—Neville Landless. Dick Datchery, the investigator who was to arrest Jasper and furnish the evidence decisive in securing his conviction, is a character based on the Scotland Yard detective Stephen Thornton.

Even Dick Tanner, one of Thornton's assistants, may provide another link connecting Mary Emsley's murder to *The Mystery of Edwin Drood.* Earlier I suggested that the name "Dick Datchery" is a Dickensian variation of "Dick Thatcher," and that Dickens based his detective's name on "Thatcher" either because it resembles Thornton, or because a thatcher thatches straw, and "Sergeant Straw" (Frederick Shaw in real life) was another detective with whom Dickens was acquainted. In poker parlance, I was sandbagging—there are at least two other ways to account for the name.

The first is that "Dick Thatcher" took his name from Dick Tanner. By the time of *Drood's* publication in 1870, Tanner had succeeded Jonathan Whicher as the most celebrated detective in England; he had won enduring fame as a result of the North London Railway murder—the first train murder (1864) in English history. When the killer, a young German named Franz Müller, fled to the United States, Tanner sailed on a faster ship and beat his quarry to New York by three weeks. By the time the murderer arrived, the extradition papers had been signed and Dick Tanner's name was a household word on both sides of the Atlantic. Not that I think for a moment that Dick Datchery is a Dickensified Dick Tanner. To the best of my knowledge Dickens never met Tanner, who in any case was not quite twelve years old when Datchery arrived in Cloisterham in mid-1843. But there is a good chance that the detective modeled on Thornton owes his name to young Dick Tanner.

The other possibility stems from the fact that Jonathan Whicher's nickname was Jack,[14] which gives us the similar-sounding Jack Whicher/Dick Thatcher. As the source for Datchery's surname, therefore, we can choose from Thornton/Thatcher, Straw/Thatcher, Tanner/Thatcher, or Whicher/

Thatcher. Whether or not all these alternatives occurred to Dickens, Datchery's name suggests a whole roster of Scotland Yard detectives!

Speaking of Dick Tanner reminds me that he was one of two famous detectives—among the best-known of their respective eras—who went into the business of tavern-keeping when their police careers ended. Suffering from rheumatism and other complaints, Tanner retired from the Metropolitan Police in July 1869 (just about the time Dickens was starting to plan *Drood*), and took the White Swan at Winchester, where he died, in 1873, at the early age of forty-one.[15] The other sleuth-turned-innkeeper was the renowned Bow Street Runner George Ruthven, who became landlord of the One Tun Tavern, Chandos Street, Covent Garden, in 1839 (the year Parliament disbanded the Runners) and ran it until his death in 1844.[16] It was Ruthven who arrested John Thurtell, Dickens's "best remembered" murderer, for killing William Weare. Perhaps these real-life models inspired the author to give his two most outstanding detectives a "tavern connection": Inspector Bucket mentions (in Chapter 53 of *Bleak House*) that his father ended his working life as an innkeeper, and Dick Datchery tells us (in Chapter 23 of *Edwin Drood)* that he likes "the old tavern way of keeping scores."

While the cases presented above had a considerable influence on the contents of *Edwin Drood,* there are other police-related incidents of equal interest that I've saved for my next chapter.

Chapter VII

A Dangerous Voyage

Other events from actual police cases may shed light on some of the unexplained mysteries in *Edwin Drood,* if we view them from the perspective that Dick Datchery is a Scotland Yard officer, rather than one of the book's other characters hiding under a white wig. Take, for instance, this oft-quoted passage from Chapter 23: "John Jasper's lamp is kindled, and his lighthouse is shining when Mr. Datchery returns alone toward it. As mariners on a dangerous voyage, approaching an iron-bound coast, may look along the beams of the warning light to the haven lying beyond it that may never be reached, so Mr. Datchery's wistful gaze is directed to this beacon, and beyond."

If Datchery is a professional detective, why exactly is his assignment referred to as "a dangerous voyage"? Ascertaining what this phrase means will simultaneously clear up another problem: Why did Dickens wait "full half a year" after Edwin's disappearance to send his secret agent to Cloisterham?

The answer to both questions hinges upon our recognition of the spectre that haunts every detective: *the fear of failure.* Sometimes the effects of failure are negligible, but often they can be devastating. Two cases where the detectives failed and lived to laugh about it are reported in Dickens's *Household Words* articles "The Detective Police" and "Three

The Police Find Patrick O'Connor's Body

'Detective' Anecdotes." The seven short tales in these articles were selected by the detectives themselves, or by Dickens, to make his heroes look good; yet in two of the seven the detective fails. In "The Adventures of a Carpet Bag" Sergeant Dornton (Stephen Thornton) traces the bill-stealer Aaron Mesheck "to Cheltenham, to Birmingham, to Liverpool, to the Atlantic Ocean. At Liverpool he was too many for me. He had gone to the United States, and I gave up all thoughts of Mesheck, and likewise of his—Carpet Bag." True, Dornton later comes across the fugitive in a New York prison, but it was not the English detective who put him there.

In "A Pair of Gloves" Inspector Wield very cleverly tracks down the owner of some gloves found at the scene of Eliza Grimwood's murder, but the young man easily establishes his innocence. Neither Wield (Charles Frederick Field) nor Dickens mentions this crucial point: Eliza Grimwood was a real murder victim whose killer was never apprehended.

Not surprisingly, these failures are treated very lightly in *Household Words.* But failure had a darker side, as two famous cases demonstrate. The first involved an ambitious young police sergeant named Popay, whose sad story can be found in just about every history of Scotland Yard published to date.[1] In 1833 the Home Secretary, becoming concerned about the activities of a radical group known as the National Political Union, asked the Commissioners of the Metropolitan Police (which had been established just four years before) to assign someone to keep an eye on these agitators. Sergeant Popay, a former schoolteacher who was regarded by his superiors as exceptionally intelligent, was chosen for this assignment. It has never been revealed precisely what instructions Popay received, but he attacked his task with enthusiasm, disguising himself as a bohemian artist and telling his new friends in the National Political Union how much he detested the Metropolitan Police! Soon Popay officially joined the

Union, and (according to some historians) made incendiary speeches and even became one of its leaders. As a trusted insider, Popay was able to learn everything the police wanted to know about the Union's plans and activities. There is no mention anywhere that his superiors criticized his methods in getting this information.

At least, there was no criticism until he was exposed as a spy. One day another member of the Union, passing by a police station, looked in through the window and saw his friend Popay talking pleasantly with the policemen he supposedly despised. When the newspapers got hold of the story (as they soon did), the affair exploded into a national scandal. And with good reason. When Sir Robert Peel had proposed setting up his New Police, many thoughtful Englishmen objected that such a force would undermine the Constitution; that an efficient English police would soon degenerate into a network of paid political spies like their counterparts across the Channel. The revelation of Popay's duplicity confirmed these fears: just four short years after Peel's Act was passed, an agent provocateur was being employed to spy on freeborn Englishmen!

Soon a Select Committee was set up by Parliament to investigate the matter. The joint Commissioners, Colonel Charles Rowan and Mr. Richard Mayne, were called on the carpet and had to devote days of testimony to justify the employment of policemen in plain clothes. In the end, the Commissioners were exonerated and were even permitted to continue the use of plainclothes officers. Of course, the Committee "solemnly deprecated an approach to the employment of spies—'a practice most abhorrent to the feelings of the people and most alien to the spirit of the Constitution'—but at the same time they held that 'the system as laid down by the heads of the police department affords no matter of complaint while confined to detecting breaches of the law.' "[2]

But what of Sergeant Popay, the young officer with a promising police career before him when the affair started? He was summarily dismissed from the force. The fate of one insignificant policeman was nothing to Commissioners Rowan and Mayne, whose sole concern was the reputation—and in fairness, the very existence—of the new organization entrusted to their leadership. A scapegoat was needed, and the buck stopped with Sergeant Popay.

It would be interesting to learn with which side Dickens sympathized in this affair. As a youthful "radical" he may have approved of the aims of the National Political Union; but as a 21-year-old Parliamentary reporter eager to rise in the world, he must have felt some sense of identification with the ambitious young police sergeant.

The second case was even more renowned in its day; then known as the Road Hill or Road Murder, it is now generally called "The Case of Constance Kent." On the morning of June 30, 1860, four-year-old Francis Saville Kent was found dead in an outhouse with his head almost severed from his body. After a two-week delay, which gave the murderer time to destroy some vital evidence, the Trowbridge magistrates asked the Home Secretary for the assistance of a Metropolitan Police detective. Richard Mayne (now Sir Richard and sole Commissioner, Colonel Rowan having retired in 1850) selected for this assignment a man with the reputation as the best detective at Scotland Yard: Jonathan Whicher, whom one of his younger colleagues later called "the prince of detectives."[3] Inspector Whicher arrived at the town of Road on July 15, and on July 20 he arrested the person his investigation had convinced him was guilty—Constance Kent, the 16-year-old half-sister of the victim. But Whicher was able to find no concrete evidence to prove her guilt, for Constance had already burned the nightdress she wore when she killed her little brother. At the magistrate's examination, Constance's defense counsel heaped abuse on Whicher for accusing an "innocent" young girl, and the newspapers (with only a few exceptions) followed his lead and viciously attacked the detective. Perhaps Whicher could have endured their calumny, but what really hurt was that he had lost the confidence of Sir Richard Mayne,[4] who now assigned the most important investigations to other men. Whicher's brilliant reputation was destroyed by this single case; when he retired a few years later, still a comparatively young man, the justification given for his early retirement was "mental depression."[5]

These two cases, and others like them, made clear to the officers themselves and to an interested observer like Charles Dickens that a detective who failed was not likely to receive much support or sympathy from headquarters. On the contrary, one conspicuous blunder could result in humiliation, disgrace, or dismissal—and sometimes all three.

With this information in hand, we return to the questions raised above concerning events in *The Mystery of Edwin Drood.* The reason why Sergeant Datchery (as we'll call him for convenience) gazes wistfully at John Jasper's window, like a mariner on a dangerous voyage, should now be clear. Mr. Jasper, the choirmaster of Cloisterham Cathedral, seems to be the model of a thoroughly respectable English gentleman, and *Datchery is spying on this paragon of respectability.* Even worse, Jasper is a clever, resourceful foe; if he exposes the spy and convinces those in authority of his own innocence, then the detective will find himself in serious trouble. Edwin Drood disappeared in December, 1842,[6] just nine short years after Sergeant Popay was dismissed from the force for spying. Thus Datchery, if he loses the dangerous game in which he's engaged, can expect to suffer the same fate as those other officers who incurred the Commissioners' disapprobation. (The precarious nature of his assignment helps explain why Datchery chalks up a long, thick line inside his cupboard after the Princess Puffer boasts about knowing Jasper "Better far than all the Reverend Parsons put together know him"—the detective has just learned that the choirmaster is not quite so respectable as he at first appeared.)

What about the six-month delay between Drood's disappearance and Datchery's arrival in Cloisterham? This actually involves two separate questions: (1) Why does Dickens want such a break in the action? and (2) How will this gap be explained in the story itself? In other words, what reason would Mr. Grewgious have given (had the novel been completed) for waiting six months before sending in Datchery?

Durdles's prophetic "ghost sounds," which he heard on the Christmas Eve preceding Jasper's unaccountable expedition, and Edwin's disappearance on the Christmas Eve following it, together suggest that Jasper was to confront his enemies on the next Christmas Eve, exactly one year after his nephew vanished.[7] Now, a sharp Scotland Yard detective would hardly need a whole year to gather evidence against the murderer; six months would give him plenty of time. Besides, Datchery has to arrive in the summer when the weather is warm so he can sit with his door open, watching the thoroughfare outside Jasper's gatehouse. In short, I believe that Dickens's main reason for delaying the introduction of Datchery was simply to accommodate the timing of events in his story. If my explanation seems a bit tame, Richard Baker has another reasonably plausible hypothesis: Dickens delayed in order to give the quicklime in the tomb time to disfigure Edwin's body "so artfully" as to render identification impossible.[8]

Of course, Grewgious could hardly justify waiting to assign Datchery to the investigation by declaring, "I decided to wrap up Jasper on Christmas Eve," or worse yet, "I wanted to give the lime more time." Here again the Popay case provides a rationale that makes sense in the context of the story. Before putting a spy on Jasper, Grewgious (who after all was a lawyer) wanted to be certain that a crime had been committed. Thus he waited for Edwin's birthday in May, or possibly for his scheduled departure for Egypt in June, before taking this measure against the suspected murderer. Had Drood been alive, he would surely have returned to claim his inheritance. Because he did not return, his absence constituted the kind of presumptive evidence of death that could be presented at a magistrate's examination or a coroner's inquest. Sergeant Datchery, remembering the fate of his colleague Popay, would naturally have insisted upon some such indication of homicide before consenting to spy on the choirmaster.

As we have seen, Datchery's voyage is dangerous and his arrival in Cloisterham was delayed for six months because of the uncertainty surrounding Edwin's fate. Until the detective can prove Drood is dead, Jasper holds the upper hand.

Chapter VIII

Artistically Tenable

Most critics in discussing *The Mystery of Edwin Drood* contemptuously dismiss the hypothesis that Dick Datchery is a professional detective with one or two brief sentences to the effect that such an identification is "artistically untenable." To understand what they really mean by this phrase, it is necessary to delve beneath the ostensible reasons for their rejection of the detective theory and to expose the actual basis for their opposition.

Their first objection simply reflects the ingrained snobbery of many critics. They see police officers as members of a class beneath their own, and refuse to identify their hero Datchery with this lower class. This quote from Montagu Saunders is typical: "That [Datchery] was a detective in the ordinary sense, and similar to Dickens's other detective characters, is disproved by the internal evidence, as Datchery is an educated gentleman, a very 'diplomatic bird,' and a kind-hearted man."[1] Therefore he cannot possibly belong to the police, who (Saunders implies) are, or at least were in Dickens's day, a bunch of ignorant, cold-hearted louts.

A phrase-by-phrase analysis of Saunders's statement discloses several flaws in his interpretation of the "internal evidence." As for Datchery's being an "educated gentleman," we find no trace in his speech, aside from his use of grammatical English, of a higher education. He quotes no classics, speaks no foreign languages, and reveals no knowledge beyond that of any well-informed newspaper reader. While Stephen Thornton, my candidate as the model for Dick Datchery, was probably not a "gentleman" in Montagu Saunders's sense of that term, it is surely possible for an intelligent man with an ear for language—even someone clad in a blue uniform—to acquire a reasonable command of his mother tongue despite the lack of a formal education. Ironically, Datchery's creator did not have a university education, and he was not considered a "gentleman" by many of his contemporaries. Following Saunders's reasoning, Dickens himself would not have qualified for the role of the white-haired stranger.

Luckily, we know Dickens considered it possible to find an educated policeman because he said as much just a few years before he wrote *Edwin Drood.* In the short story "The Signal-man" (1866), the narrator, in conversation with the railroad signalman of the title, comments: "On my trusting that he would excuse the remark that he had been well educated, and (I hoped I might say without offense), perhaps educated above that station, he observed that instances of slight incongruity in such wise would rarely be found wanting among large bodies of men; that he had heard it was so in workhouses, *in the police force,* even in that last desperate resource, the army" (emphasis added).[2]

Furthermore, by the time Dickens wrote *The Mystery of Edwin Drood* in 1870, the concept of the gentleman police-detective had been firmly established by a journalist and "miscellaneous writer" named William Russell, who employed a device used earlier by "Thomas Richmond" and later by such writers as "Nick Carter" and "Ellery Queen"—he adopted as his nom de plume the same name he gave his detective. In Russell's case the name was "Waters," and the character was a gentleman who had gambled away his fortune and was forced in desperation to accept a post in the recently formed Metropolitan Police. Russell introduced Waters in the July 28, 1849, issue of *Chambers's Edinburgh Review,* and his short stories there were such a success that they were soon collected and published in America (1852) and in England (1856) under the title *The Recollections of a Detective Police-Officer.*

So well received was this volume that Russell, for the rest of his career employing the pseudonym Waters, continued to churn out such titles as *The Autobiography of an English Detective* (1863) and *The Experiences of a Real Detective* (also 1863). The last-named collection recounts the cases of Inspector F (a purely fictional hero, despite the title), who like Waters was a gentleman down on his luck; when F's business went into decline because he spent too much time on amateur sleuthing, Colonel Rowan recruited him into the New Police. Like Datchery, both Waters and F speak and write perfectly acceptable middle-class English; unlike Datchery, neither is a clearly delineated personality. Whatever his limitations as a writer, however, William Russell's books were immensely popular in his lifetime, and he made the gentleman detective-officer, whether or not such existed in real life, a conventional literary type.

Besides dubbing Datchery "an educated gentleman," Saunders suggests that a professional detective lacks the capacity to assume the role of a "diplomatic bird"—i.e., one skilled in the arts of diplomacy. As a matter of fact, Scotland Yard officers regularly traveled to France and the United States on police business, usually to conduct negotiations with the authorities in these countries for the extradition of fugitives from justice. In "The Detective Police," Sergeant Dornton (Stephen Thornton) relates how he pursued an Irish swindler named Doctor Dundey to America, and how, after "a deal of artifice and trouble," he managed to arrest Dundey and take him before a magistrate in New York City. At the request of the Polish government, Inspector Jonathan Whicher was sent to Warsaw in the 1850's to set up a detective department similar to the one in London.[3] In short, Metropolitan Police detectives had considerable functional experience in the practice of diplomacy; certainly more than such tyros as Edwin, Helena, and Neville, and probably more than the sailor Tartar, the law-clerk Bazzard, or even the old rent-collector Grewgious.

Another true detective story tends to confirm this point. In March, 1840, Scotland Yard learned that Prince Louis Napoleon and the Comte Leon were planning to fight a duel on Wimbledon Common. Duelling by this time being illegal, Inspector Nicholas Pearce and several of his subordinates were assigned to prevent the duel and arrest the participants—which the officers did, taking the entire party into custody "with the deference due to the nobility even when they were committing a criminal act."[4] Well! If Inspector Pearce could be trusted to handle a Prince and a Count (the genuine article, too, not your *Huck Finn* variety), then surely Sergeant Datchery could convince the provincials of Cloisterham that diplomacy was or had been his profession.

Saunders's last nugget of internal evidence is his assertion that Dick Datchery is "a kind-hearted man." Richard Proctor agrees; to him, Datchery is "quaint, humorous, genial, and kindly."[5] Yet consider this fact: every act of kindness that Datchery performs is in some way self-serving. When he befriends young Deputy, sending many of his sixpences the boy's way, he gets an ample return for his investment—a very capable assistant. Similarly, while he treats the Princess Puffer with tolerant good humor and gives her three-and-sixpence to buy her "medicine," he is well repaid in useful information. Here again we find a close parallel to Inspector Bucket of the Detective. Bucket seems kindly disposed toward Jo, the poor crossing-sweep, but he ruthlessly "moves the boy on" when it suits his purpose; and the inspector's arrest of trooper George is a model of solicitous courtesy, but the detective gets what he wants: George submits to arrest without a murmur (*BH,* Chapter 49).

Thus Datchery does not deserve to be called "kind-hearted" because kind deeds reveal a kind heart only when they are not actuated by self-interest. Perhaps by the end of *Edwin Drood* (had it been completed) Dick would have carried out some kindness for its own sake, as Bucket does in his treatment of the dying Gridley (*BH,* Chapter 24), but he has not passed this test at the point where the story breaks off.

Enough said about Montagu Saunders. W. Robertson Nicoll rejects the notion that Datchery is a professional detective, or in fact any new character, because to him it is poor form to introduce a major personality so late in the novel.[6] As we've already seen in my chapter on latecomers, Dickens brought belated characters into his stories more often than not, generally introducing such stragglers at the point where his plot necessitates their appearance. Thus his detectives consistently arrive on the scene when a crime occurs or some other mystery requires an investigator: Blathers and Duff show up in *Oliver Twist* (Chapter 31) shortly after an attempted burglary, the Bow Street Runners in *Great Expectations* (Chapter 16) after the attack on Mrs. Joe Gargery, the Night Inspector in *Our Mutual Friend* (Chapter 3) after a body has been fished out of the Thames, and Sergeant Datchery in *Edwin Drood* after Edwin's disappearance. As Edwin vanishes at the end of Chapter 14 and Datchery does not enter until the beginning of Chapter 18, Dickens was obviously not concerned about the old buffer's late arrival; in fact there is evidence that he was worried about bringing him into the novel too soon.[7]

Dickens introduced his two most important detectives (before Datchery), Nadgett of *Martin Chuzzlewit* and Inspector Bucket of *Bleak House,* when he needed someone to investigate not crimes but "private inquiries of a delicate nature," although in both cases the author had a murder in prospect. Both Nadgett and Bucket are brought into the narrative at a fairly advanced point in the story's progress; both could have been introduced earlier had Dickens actually believed that the late appearance of major characters violated some essential artistic canon. (Bucket for example could have been mentioned as Tulkinghorn's agent as early as Chapter 10, when the lawyer starts his campaign against Lady Dedlock.) The same can be said of such non-detective characters as Lieutenant Tartar, Edith Granger, and Dora Spenlow, all of whom could have been presented much sooner in their respective novels. That Dickens did not mention any of them earlier proves that the "rule" against late introductions was invented by Nicoll and others after the author's death; there is no evidence it was followed by Dickens himself at any stage of his career.

The next objection to the "detective theory" comes from those who, like Richard A. Proctor and J. Cuming Walters, regard the "Datchery Assumption" as the most important of the novel's secrets, and who therefore expect the revelation of Dick's true identity to provide the climax of the story. To such critics it is essential that Datchery should be a major character like Edwin Drood or Helena Landless, whose unmasking would supposedly astonish most readers. Naturally enough, I disagree entirely with this proposition; it is not who Datchery is, *but what he was going to do,* that was intended to provide the fireworks. As Aubrey Boyd so perceptively writes, "Dickens regarded the identity of Datchery as a feature of minor interest in his story, necessary to sustain the suspense until the really extraordinary climax and denouement, and no more. . . . [Datchery's] resolution to track the crime to Jasper's door is perfectly apparent from the first. . . . His incognito character is equally apparent, and the question of his true identity is subordinate to the real perplexity in the reader's mind as to how Jasper is to be brought to justice. . . . The only thing unknown about Datchery is his right name, and however intriguing this may be in itself, it could never be made the determining factor of the story."[8]

There is another and more compelling reason why stripping Datchery of his disguise cannot furnish the novel's denouement. If it did, Dickens could not possibly have filled up the second half of his book, which required six more installments, consisting of approximately twenty-two more chapters, to fulfill his commitment to his publishers and his public. A brief outline of the plot, and a little simple arithmetic, will demonstrate my point. Here is what remains to be accomplished if exposing Datchery provides the final climax of the story:

1. Datchery has to find the place where Drood's body was concealed after the assault. When the novel breaks off, Dick is just on the verge of doing so; he has made contact with Durdles, Deputy, and the Opium Woman, one or more of whom will lead him to the Sapsea tomb. Unless Datchery is a complete bungler, it should take him no more than *three chapters* to locate Drood's sepulchre. (Even these few chapters are superfluous if Drood himself is Datchery, or if he's working with the investigator, because Edwin living ought to know where his intended grave was located.)

2. Someone, probably Bazzard, has to tell Jasper about the engagement ring to entice the choirmaster to return to the place of concealment. Allow *one chapter* at most for this revelation.

3. Jasper has to go to the tomb to be confronted by Datchery (whoever he is). *One chapter.*

4. His enemies have to pursue Jasper up the tower stairs and arrest him. *One chapter.*

5. Jasper has to be tried and convicted, and he has to confess in his condemned cell. As these events are all post-climactic in this version of the plot, they require at most *two chapters.*

6. Finally, there has to be a wrap-up chapter or *two* (surely no more) to marry off the eligible suitors and satisfactorily dispose of the other characters.

Adding up these estimates yields a maximum of just *ten chapters*—about a dozen chapters short of the projected total. Unless Dickens was prepared to pad shamefully the second half of his book—which is unlikely, as the extant portion is as tightly written and expertly crafted as anything he ever wrote—then he must have had some truly significant developments in store for us *after Jasper's arrest.* And if he did, there is a lot more to the story than the mere unraveling of the Datchery assumption could provide.

The last and most important reason why critics deride the professional-detective theory is their unspoken and perhaps unconscious conviction that if Datchery is a new character then his identity is hopelessly undiscoverable, and that as a result *The Mystery* must remain forever unsolved. Therefore they insist on applying to *Edwin Drood* one of the rules of the modern whodunit: namely that the party whose identity is being sought (usually the murderer, but in *Drood,* Datchery) has to be one of a group of potential suspects previously introduced into the story. But there is absolutely no evidence that Dickens followed this rule, any more than that he felt bound by the early-introduction rule, or that he believed his readers would be offended by the disclosure that Datchery was a professional detective. To state the point in another way, critics who reject the professional-detective theory believe that such a revelation would be unfair to the novel's readers in general and to themselves in particular. But are they right? Or could an astute reader of 1870 have figured out Dick Datchery's identity either from hints in the book itself (had it been completed) or from evidence external to the novel?

It is a fallacy to suppose that all the clues Dickens intended to include have already been presented in the half-finished novel. On the contrary, he had plenty of time to plant additional pointers as the story progressed. For example, there is a fragmentary clue that Dickens started but died before completing, which would have instantly alerted perceptive readers to Dick Datchery's occupational status as a police officer. The first element of this clue was presented in Chapter 8, where Dickens writes of Septimus Crisparkle: "The Minor Canon props [Neville] by the elbow with a strong hand (in a strictly scientific manner, worthy of his morning trainings), and turns him into his own little book-room. . . . Scooping his hand into the same elbow-rest as before, and backing it up with the inert strength of his arm, *as skilfully as a Police Expert,* and with an apparent repose quite unattainable by novices, Mr. Crisparkle conducts his pupil to the pleasant and orderly old room prepared for him" (emphasis added).

As it happens, this "hand on the elbow" grip was a favorite policeman's technique with Dickens. As early as *The Old Curiosity Shop* the police constable who arrests Kit (in Chapter 60) holds the boy "carelessly by the arm, a little above the elbow." A few paragraphs later, "the constable, still holding Kit in the same manner, and pushing him on a little before him, so as to keep him at about three-quarters of an arm's length in advance (which is the professional mode), thrust him into the vehicle and followed himself." And in Chapter 22 of *Bleak House,* in order to escort Jo to Tulkinghorn's office, "Mr. Bucket has to take Jo by the arm a little above the elbow and walk him on before him; without which observance, neither the Tough Subject nor any other Subject could be professionally conducted to Lincoln's Inn Fields."

So what was the point of using this "professional hold" in *Edwin Drood?* The Reverend Septimus is not, and never was, a police officer. Nor can Crisparkle be Datchery; on the penultimate page of the *Drood* fragment, the two men are together at the same time in the same place—the Cathedral. No, Dickens gave a precise description of the scientific grip so that later it would be recognized *when Datchery used the same grip on someone else*—say Durdles or Sapsea or the Opium Woman—and thereby informed attentive readers that he was one of Dickens's policemen.

Facts external to the novel tend to direct the knowledgeable reader to the same conclusion. In the years from 1842 through 1863 there were only eight officers assigned to the Detective Department at Scotland Yard: two inspectors and six sergeants. As late as 1870, when Charles Dickens died, there were only fifteen detectives, three of them inspectors, at headquarters, in a force of eight thousand men.[9] In those days police news enjoyed much more press coverage than it does today. A sensational murder was reported in niggling and sometimes nauseous detail; if the killer was apprehended, the record of his trial was published virtually verbatim; and if he was convicted, whole columns were devoted to his behavior in jail and his last moments on the scaffold. Consequently the names of the two or three Scotland Yard inspectors, who headed every major investigation, repeatedly appeared in newspaper accounts of notable crimes, and must have been thoroughly familiar to their contemporaries.

Dickens was certainly aware of the detectives' notoriety and helped contribute to it when in 1850–1851 he and W. H. Wills published their "detective" articles in *Household Words.* For the first of these articles, "A Detective Police Party" (1850), Dickens interviewed seven of the detectives in his editorial office in the Strand, London. After discussing other topics, he and his guests glided "into a review of the most celebrated and horrible of the great crimes that have been committed within the last fifteen or twenty years. The men engaged in the discovery of almost all of them, and in the pursuit or apprehension of the murderers, are here, down to the very last instance." Small wonder that this undermanned staff was famous throughout Great Britain.

One of the seven officers at Dickens's "detective party" was Stephen Thornton, who had been a charter member of the Detective Department when it was created in 1842, and who continued to serve therein, as sergeant and inspector, until his retirement in 1863. Those who regularly followed the newspaper police reports should have been able to recognize Datchery's similarities to Thornton if sufficient clues were provided in *Edwin Drood.* Besides, Dickens would have assumed that his more faithful readers had read his *Household Words* articles about the detectives, especially since these articles had been reissued in *Reprinted Pieces,* and that they would also spot Datchery's family likeness to Dornton.

Those who read the popular fiction of the years immediately preceding *Drood's* publication would also have expected a detective, and most likely a Scotland Yard detective, to turn up in Dickens's last novel, for the 1860's can truly be called "The Decade of the Detectives." The stories of "Waters," published in magazines and reprinted in collections, have already been mentioned. Working the same vein were such short-story writers as Charles Martel (Thomas Delf), Andrew Forrester Jr., William S. Hayward, Charles Hillyard, Robert Curtis, John B. Williams, James McGovan, William Henderson, Tom Fox (John Bennett),[10] and Samuel Warren. On the stage, playwright Tom Taylor scored an enormous triumph with his drama *The Ticket-of-Leave Man* (1863), which featured a Scotland Yard sleuth whose name is still used as a synonym for members of his calling—Hawkshaw the detective.

Novels like Mary Elizabeth Braddon's *Henry Dunbar* (1864), John Berwick Harwood's *Lady Flavia* (1866), and Charles Felix's *Notting Hill Mystery* (1865) also employed Scotland Yard detectives; and in *Lost Sir Massingberd* (1864) James Payn resurrected the historical Bow Street Runner John Townsend (spelled "Townshend" by Payn) to trace his missing Massingberd. One of the greatest of all mystery novels, Wilkie Collins's *The Moonstone* (1868) was published in this same decade (in Dickens's *All the Year Round,* as a matter of fact); and Collins's brilliant creation Sergeant Richard Cuff, still another Scotland Yard officer,[11] owed much of his method to the real Inspector Jonathan Whicher of "Constance Kent" fame. While Cuff bears almost no physical resemblance to Whicher, contemporary readers recognized immediately the connection between the two, because a stained nightgown played a major part in Cuff's search for the Moonstone, as one had in Whicher's famous murder case. Since Wilkie Collins has been permitted to utilize a professional detective without drawing charges of artistic dereliction, why shouldn't Dickens be accorded the same privilege?

Ironically, in the years immediately following the publication of *Edwin Drood* the professional-detective theory had some articulate champions,[12] a fact which suggests that in Dickens's own time readers sensed Datchery's definite if elusive resemblance to Inspector Bucket and his fellow detectives. But between them Richard Proctor and John Cuming Walters, two very persuasive writers, sold the idea that Dick must be a character previously presented, and as the years rolled by and their theories came to saddle the Datchery assumption with the whodunit hypothesis, the common-sense identification of Dick Datchery as a professional detective has been steadily buried under layers of eloquent but specious prose.

Chapter IX

The Professional Touch

In a letter dated 6 January 1914, another very persuasive writer named George Bernard Shaw expressed his opinion about Datchery's identity to B. W. Matz, then editor of *The Dickensian:* "I have just read Edwin Drood carefully through. Datchery wasnt anybody in disguise: he was a detective of the Bucket or Sergeant Cuff (Wilkie Collins) type."[1]

Judging from this statement, Shaw's opinion was not the product of any extensive research on his part; rather, it was based solely on his reading of Dickens's novel. What is there about Dick Datchery's behavior that would lead an observant reader to this conclusion?

Whenever he appears onstage, Mr. Datchery invariably conducts himself like someone who has had considerable experience as an investigator. His every move demonstrates how well prepared he is for his assignment in Cloisterham, and how confident he feels in his handling of it.

We first meet the white-haired stranger in the coffee-room of the Crozier Hotel, where he tells the waiter to look inside his hat to see what is written there. The waiter reads the single word "Datchery," and the gentleman responds, "Now you know my name, Dick Datchery." Very few readers believe that this is the stranger's real name. Some think he is Drood or Bazzard or Tartar, or one of the other characters in the story; some like me think he is a professional detective working under an alias; but whoever he is, he has had the foresight to have his pseudonym printed inside his hat. In our day and age, an investigator working undercover would secure a counterfeit driver's license to establish his false identity; but in Dickens's time the name in the hat served the same purpose—it cemented the pseudonym as an indisputable fact in the minds of those whom Dick wanted to deceive. For who would be likely to question a name that he saw inscribed in a person's hat?

Datchery's next move is to find a suitable lodging for himself. "Suitable" in this context has a special meaning. As the site from which he intends to stake out the choirmaster's quarters, his new lodging has to be located as close to Jasper's as possible. Whether he is another character in disguise or a detective hired by Grewgious, Dick already knows that Jasper lives in the Cathedral gatehouse. Quite possibly he also knows that Mr. and Mrs. Tope have a set of ideally situated rooms to let. Accordingly he could make his way to the gatehouse and look for lodgings without quizzing the waiter for suggestions. Yet Dick takes pains to solicit the waiter's help. In fact, when that worthy fails to catch his drift, Datchery prompts him with, "Anything Cathedraly, now." The waiter at last takes the hint and mentions the rooms advertised by the Topes.

Why has Datchery bothered to get the waiter's recommendation? So that when Mrs. Tope or John Jasper asks him, "How did you ever find this out-of-the-way place?" he can truthfully reply, "The waiter at the Crozier recommended it." And if perchance Jasper later checks out this statement, the waiter will confirm Datchery's story. My friends, this kind of advance planning is the hallmark of a professional.

After leaving the Crozier, Datchery sets out for the Cathedral and on his way encounters the stone-throwing urchin

Deputy. Instantly recognizing in the boy a potentially valuable ally, Dick begins the process of recruiting him as his assistant (which he has completed successfully when we meet them again in Chapter 23). One can readily accept a team consisting of an experienced detective and a dirty street Arab (with Datchery and Deputy anticipating Sherlock Holmes and his Baker Street Irregulars), but it's hard to swallow the notion that a youngster like Edwin or Neville, or a young lady like Helena, would choose to work with such an obstreperous little ruffian.

With Deputy's help, Datchery finds Mr. and Mrs. Tope's dwelling, where he surveys the chambers they have to let, and agrees to take the rooms then and there "on condition that reference was permitted him to Mr. Jasper" to verify their respectability. Surely this is the most amazing request that any Dickens character ever made. Probably there was no couple in England more respectable-looking than the verger and his comely wife. Besides, the chambers in question are perfectly positioned to conduct his surveillance of Jasper's rooms, so of course Dick will take them regardless of anything Jasper may have to say about the Topes.

What then is the real reason for Datchery's strange request? Clearly he must make Jasper's acquaintance *before* he assumes his post at the open door of his suite, "eyeing all who pass, as if he were toll-taker of the gateway—though the way is free." If the choirmaster came home one night and found a complete stranger staring at him curiously as he went up to his rooms, he might guess the newcomer's intentions. So Datchery allays any suspicion in advance by making himself known to Jasper as a harmless old eccentric before he moves into his new chambers.

When Mrs. Tope asks Datchery if he has heard something of Edwin's disappearance, "Mr. Datchery had as confused a knowledge of the event in question, on trying to recall it, as he well could have. He begged Mrs. Tope's pardon when she found it incumbent on her to correct him in every detail of his summary of the facts." Here Datchery is pumping the good lady for information in the most approved detective fashion. By feeding her a series of misstatements to correct, he is able to draw her out without appearing to have the slightest personal interest in the Drood affair.

We find more evidence of Datchery's experience in his masterful handling of such disparate types as Mr. Sapsea and the Princess Puffer, whose characters he reads at a glance and whose frailties he skillfully exploits. The Mayor's predominant foibles being "self-sufficient stupidity and conceit," Datchery shamelessly flatters the old dunderhead to gain his confidence and cooperation. As for the Opium Woman, Dick quickly observes that her characteristic vice is greed, and (by rattling the loose coins in his pockets, taking out his money and slowly counting it from hand to hand, pretending he has counted wrong and starting again, and so forth) he plays upon this weakness to pry out of her as much as he safely can in a first interview.

Displaying his habitual presence of mind, he manages (without calling attention to the fact) to accompany the Puffer far enough on her way back to her inn to perceive she is staying at the Traveller's Twopenny, where his friend Deputy is employed. That same evening he directs the boy to find out exactly where in London she lives, so that he can question her further at his convenience. (Earlier, Dick had seized the opportunity of his chance introduction to the stonemason Durdles to arrange another meeting with him in the privacy of his home. Note how promptly and efficiently he acts at all times to advance his investigation.)

On returning to his chambers, Datchery refers to an uncouth tally, "Illegible except to the scorer," chalked up inside his cupboard door. The point of this whimsical scoreboard would be lost on someone who had never experienced the tedium of surveillance. It is simply a device adopted by an old pro as an antidote to boredom.

A final clue to Dick's calling may be found in his reaction to one of the Mayor's bombastic pronouncements. Shortly after leaving Jasper's rooms Datchery inquires about the loss of Edwin Drood, and in the course of the discussion Mr. Sapsea remarks, "It is not enough that Justice should be morally certain; she must be immorally certain—legally, that is."

To which Mr. Datchery responds, "His Honour reminds me of the nature of the law. Immoral. How true!" Some have inferred from this comment that Dick is a lawyer, but it seems to me that a member of the bar (particularly one created by Charles Dickens) would be the last person to criticize the handiwork of the legal profession. On the other hand, a gibe at the law's shortcomings would be entirely appropriate from a policeman, who sometimes has the disagreeable task of enforcing foolish and ill-framed laws.

So how does my hypothesis about Dick Datchery's prior experience accord with the facts? I believe that his opportunistic and decisive style stamps him unmistakably as a professional investigator. To classify him as a rank amateur, as so many writers have done in the past, is to ignore his impressive display of expertise in the art of detection.

Chapter X

Surprise Endings

The central question in *The Mystery of Edwin Drood* remains to be addressed. Did John Jasper murder Edwin Drood? On this issue I hold with the majority of commentators that the choirmaster did indeed kill his nephew.[1] There are, however, two groups of critics who oppose this view. Although their conclusions differ widely, the motivation underlying the theories of both is identical: they want a *surprise ending* to the mystery.

The first group consists of those who contend that John Jasper is innocent, and that someone else murdered, or attempted to murder, Edwin Drood. While there are probably others, I've come across only three writers with the temerity to advocate Jasper's innocence. Felix Aylmer fancied that an Arab conspiracy was behind the attack on Edwin, who nevertheless managed to escape;[2] John Dickson Carr theorized that Helena, disguised as her brother Neville, killed Drood;[3] and Arthur J. Cox suggested that Neville himself murdered Edwin.[4] These three solutions share a common flaw—they are all egregiously un-Dickensian. Aylmer's tale of conspiracy, for instance, would have been virtually unsolvable because in his outline of the story every event of any significance happens offstage. Aylmer ingenuously remarks that the effect on the reader, upon learning of Jasper's innocence, would have been "a pleasant surprise" at a happy ending.[5] Most readers on the contrary would have been furious had Dickens tried to foist off on us an impossible-to-solve mystery, the ultimate expression of a writer's contempt for his readers.[6] Popular novelists please their public, and Dickens, one of the most popular who ever lived, did not conceive a story calculated to offend almost everyone who read it.

With regard to Carr and Cox, the notion that Helena or Neville Landless is the culprit runs counter to everything Dickens believed about the proper depiction of murderers and their victims. Repeatedly, he expressed the opinion that the real-life murderer gets too much attention and sympathy, the victim not nearly enough.[7] As Philip Collins says, Dickens "had always shared the common assumption that murderers are, by temperament, monsters of vice. . . . For him, murderers were always wholly vile, never pitiful; one of his main objections to capital punishment, and later to public executions, was indeed that hanging a man made him too much an object for sympathy, and that a reform in the law would 'leave the general compassion to expend itself on the only theme at present quite forgotten in the history, that is to say, the murdered person.' "[8]

Half of *Edwin Drood* had been written when Charles Dickens died, and every line of the third-person narrator, presumably voicing the thoughts of the author himself, implies that Jasper is a depraved, unrepentant killer. In earlier stories Dickens had done his utmost to make the likes of Bill Sikes, Jonas Chuzzlewit, Julius Slinkton, and the rest totally reprehensible, and he obviously set out to make John Jasper equally odious. Edwin Drood, on the other hand, somehow manages to win our affection in spite of all his youthful faults. If Jasper murdered Drood, we have exactly the combination at which Dickens was aiming: a hateful villain and a victim for whom we can feel genuinely sorry. In short, Edwin is portrayed so sympathetically not because he is too good to die, but rather because his murderer was not to be forgiven for killing him.

All of which explains why neither Helena nor Neville killed Drood: they are just not vicious enough to be Dickensian murderers. If either committed the crime, our sympathy would all too surely shift from Edwin to the guilty party in his or her tribulations after being arrested. Not that Helena has any imaginable motive for killing Edwin, but even if Carr could have found one for her, it is inconceivable that Dickens would have turned his noble Amazon into a "horrible wonder apart." While Neville does have a motive of sorts, it is the kind likely to make us take his side against Drood, whose racist insult of the dark-skinned Landless shows Edwin at his worst. Besides, Mr. Crisparkle devoutly believes Neville to be innocent of Drood's murder (as he tells Honeythunder in Chapter 17), and it is as inconsistent with the minor canon's nature to misread his pupil's character as it is with Neville's to commit a premeditated murder.

The other group who deny that Jasper killed his nephew maintain that he attempted to do so, but botched the job and allowed Edwin to escape. Like those who espouse Jasper's innocence, these folks too want a surprise ending, and they think that Drood's reappearance alive in the last act will provide it.

In fact, Edwin's survival would have afforded little or no surprise to a well-read contemporary of Dickens. The years preceding *Drood's* publication yielded a heavy crop of mystery novels in which the central plot device was the disappearance of a potential victim. In some of these stories the victim dies and in others he survives, but both conclusions had been used often enough by 1870 that neither could be expected to astonish anybody. Even Dickens himself, in the five years before *Drood* was published, had thrice allowed a presumed victim to "return from the dead": John Harmon and Eugene Wrayburn in *Our Mutual Friend* (1865) and George Vendale in *No Thoroughfare* (1867, written in collaboration with Wilkie Collins).

Another book in the back-to-life category is T. W. Speight's *Under Lock and Key* (1869), in which a young husband who has tired of his wife "drowns" in a Swiss lake and reappears under another name. In its own day, however, the best-known novel with a resurrected victim was the immensely successful *Lady Audley's Secret* by Mary Elizabeth Braddon. The bigamous Lady Audley's first husband George Talboys disappears, and both the amateurish investigator, Robert Audley, and the lady herself think she's killed him; but at the end of the book George returns alive and well. *Lady Audley's Secret* was published on October 1, 1862, "and went through eight editions before the end of the year. . . . for half a century after its appearance in 1862 it was one of the most popular novels in the English-speaking world."[9]

Thackeray reportedly said of this story, "If I could plot like Miss Braddon, I should be the greatest novelist that ever lived."[10] One wonders what Dickens thought of that! Whether or not he shared Thackeray's high opinion, the Conductor of *All the Year Round* must have been aware of a book that rivaled *The Woman in White* in sales.

On the other side of the ledger, *The Disappearance of John Ackland* (1869), written by Robert Lytton and serialized in *All the Year Round; Lost Sir Massingberd* (1864) by James Payn, another contributor to Dickens's magazine; and "Mad Monkton," a novelette from Wilkie Collins's *The Queen of Hearts* (1859); all ended with the disclosure that the vanished person had indeed died. Of earlier date but still highly regarded in the 1860's was *Eugene Aram* (1832), by Dickens's good friend Edward Bulwer-Lytton, in which Walter Lester's father, missing for years, is found at last buried in a Yorkshire grave.

To avoid revealing their surprise endings, I won't discuss the plots of Joseph Sheridan Le Fanu's *Wylder's Hand* (1864), John Berwick Harwood's *Lady Flavia* (1866), and Charles Reade's *Griffith Gaunt* (1866), except to say that the title character of each of these novels disappears, and that each side of the ledger claims at least one of them.

Because a knowledgeable reader of his day would have been thoroughly familiar with fictional missing-body cases, Dickens's real problem in *Edwin Drood* was to infuse new vitality into an overworked literary form. I believe that he would have succeeded; that he had several surprises in store for us (which we'll come to later); but that Edwin's survival or his death was *not* one of them, nor did Dickens expect it to be.

While his fellow writers were churning out mystery novels, Charles Dickens catered to the popular taste for sensational entertainment by adding a new selection to his public-reading repertoire. This was the murder of Nancy by Bill Sikes from *Oliver Twist,* first presented (to a select audience) in November 1868, just a year and a half before his death. His performance of "Sikes and Nancy" tremendously excited Dickens; whenever he gave it his blood pressure rose to alarming heights, and it left him drained and prostrate. In spite of these ill effects, he continued to perform it until 8 March 1870, when he read it publicly for the last time. By this date he was well into the writing of *Edwin Drood.*

The author's epistolary comments about "Sikes and Nancy" are instructive. Thus he wrote to W. P. Frith, on 16 November 1868, "Come early in January, and see a certain friend of yours do the murder from *Oliver Twist.* It is horribly like, I am afraid! I have a vague sensation of being 'wanted' as I walk about the streets." To Mary Boyle, on 6 January

1869, "My preparations for a certain murder that I had to do last night have rendered me unfit for letter-writing these last few days. . . . The crime being completely off my mind and the blood spilled, I am (like many of my fellow criminals) in a highly edifying state to-day." And to Frederick Ouvry, on 20 January 1869, "I commit my murder again on Tuesday, the 2nd of March. . . . "[11]

Invariably in his letters Dickens ignores Bill Sikes and speaks of *himself* as the murderer. The novelist had always identified closely with his characters, but in performing "Sikes and Nancy" he carried this tendency to the point of obsession, enacting the piece with feverish excitement and afterward suffering utter prostration. Because he was planning and writing *Edwin Drood* at a time when the act of murder completely possessed his imagination, nothing could have been more natural for him than to contrive in his new story the killing of another innocent; nothing less natural than to permit the intended victim's escape. Of course, there is a difference between the coarse brutality of Sikes's crime and the meticulous precision of Jasper's, but it lies only in the method, not in the result. Drood has to die because what Dickens devised in his last plot was the kind of murder he himself would have committed had he turned his hand to it.

After a lifetime of following sensational criminal cases—from John Thurtell's murder of William Weare to Franz Müller's of Thomas Briggs—Dickens would also have realized that a failed assassination attempt just doesn't stir up much interest unless its target is someone important. Thus Edward Oxford is remembered (by historians, anyway) because he tried to shoot Queen Victoria, but I challenge my readers to name even one thwarted would-be murderer of the last hundred years whose chosen victim was an amiable nobody like Edwin Drood. Conversely, criminals who successfully consummate their murders, like John Thurtell, François Courvoisier, the Mannings, and John White Webster, often achieve the same renown as prominent entertainers—which, in a sense, they are.

It stands to reason someone as well-informed as Charles Dickens would not have sent a top-notch investigator like Dick Datchery all the way to Cloisterham to handle an offense as trifling as attempted murder.

Chapter XI

Proof of Death

It ought to be apparent, after more than a hundred years of squabbling, that the clues and hints to be found in *The Mystery of Edwin Drood* itself are not sufficient to establish whether the title character succumbed to or survived the attempt on his life; Dickens concealed his plans too well, and he died too soon, to betray his secrets in its pages. On the other hand, the statements of five witnesses (Charles Dickens the Younger, Kate Dickens Perugini, Charles A. Collins, John Forster, and Luke Fildes) who have commented upon Drood's fate since the novelist's death, have been entirely unanimous—they have all testified that poor Edwin *was* murdered by his uncle. The purpose of this chapter is to review their testimony and the other external proofs of death that have come to light over the years. For convenience, the term "Resurrectionists" will be applied to those writers who maintain that Edwin emerges alive from his ordeal.[1]

Turning first to Dickens's notes for the novel, we find he twice used the word "murder" to describe Drood's appointed end. In planning Chapter 2 he wrote: "Uncle and Nephew. Murder very far off." And for Chapter 12 he reminded himself: "Lay the ground for the manner of the murder, to come out at last." Some Resurrectionists contend that "murder" was Dickens's abbreviation for "attempted murder," but this explanation posits that one of the great masters of English prose could not find a simple word like "attack" if that was his meaning. Granted, such discarded titles as "The flight of Edwyn Drood" and "Edwin Drood in hiding" hint at the boy's escape, but in my opinion the writer conceived of these phrases as a means of concealing his real intentions. At the very time he listed them in his notes, Dickens as editor was changing the title of a Robert Lytton novel to avoid letting out the ending;[2] he would not have considered for a moment putting the solution of his own mystery on the cover of his book.

The author left another clue as to how his story would come out. Shortly before his death, his sister-in-law Georgina Hogarth "found it impossible to refrain from asking him, 'I hope you haven't really killed poor Edwin Drood?' To which he gravely replied, 'I call my book the Mystery, not the History, of Edwin Drood.' "[3] The key to this conundrum turns on the full titles of three of his earlier novels: *The Life and Adventures of Nicholas Nickleby, The Life and Adventures of Martin Chuzzlewit,* and *The Personal History of David Copperfield.* To me Dickens is saying, "As the Mystery in my title implies, Edwin is dead. If I had intended to write about his Life and Adventures, I should have called my book the History of Edwin Drood."

Charles Dickens died on June 9, 1870. Later that year, or early in 1871, the New York theatrical producer and playwright Augustin Daly wrote a letter to the author's eldest son Charles (or Charley, as his family called him). Daly planned to write and produce a dramatic version of *The Mystery of Edwin Drood,* and, wanting his adaptation to be as authentic as possible, he asked for any general information Charley might have concerning his father's intentions for ending the story. Disappointingly, "Young MR. DICKENS replied that the 'Mystery of Edwin Drood' was 'as great a mystery to him as it was to the public at large.' "[4]

This setback deterred Daly only briefly. Reasoning that the artist who drew the cover for the monthly parts from Dickens's own instructions might have some inside information about those cover scenes that had not yet appeared in the printed text, he wrote to Luke Fildes, the illustrator who had prepared the book's interior drawings. Fildes replied, "Mr. Charles Collins, the late Mr. Dickens' son-in-law, is the gentleman who made the design (for the cover), and in referring you to him I have no doubt you will be able to get information to your satisfaction."[5] (Both Fildes and young Dickens subsequently claimed that Charles Dickens had confided to them some information about the ending of *The Mystery;* we'll consider their later comments in due course.)

Following up the lead provided by Fildes, Daly next wrote to Charles Allston Collins, designer of the parts cover, husband of Dickens's daughter Kate, and brother of the author's good friend and occasional collaborator Wilkie Collins. Charles Collins's reply was dated May 4, 1871, less than a year after Dickens's death and only eighteen months after the artist had executed the cover design. "The late Mr. Dickens communicated to me some general outlines for his scheme of 'Edwin Drood' . . . " Collins wrote, and continued without a trace of uncertainty, "Edwin Drood was *never to re-appear,* he having been murdered by Jasper. . . . It was intended that Jasper himself should urge on the search after Edwin Drood and the pursuit of his murderer, thus endeavoring to direct suspicion from himself, the real murderer. This is indicated in the design on the right side of the cover of the figures hurrying up the spiral staircase, emblematical of a pursuit. They are led on by Jasper, who points unconsciously to his own figure in the drawing at the head of the title."[6] Note especially the last two sentences of this passage. Clearly what the artist gives us here is a paraphrase or even a direct quote of Charles Dickens's actual instructions to his illustrator. How else could Collins have been so sure that the figure pointing to Jasper is Jasper himself?

Under the title "The 'Mystery' Solved," Augustin Daly published, in the *Bill of the Play for the Fifth Avenue Theatre* dated September 5, 1871, a brief account of his correspondence with Dickens Junior, Fildes, and Charles Collins. In this article he introduced Collins's reply with the significant prefatory comment that, "as the letter has its own unique literary interest and value, MR. DALY presents it here without abridgement."[7] Because a playbill tends to disappear almost immediately into oblivion, Daly's information about *Edwin Drood* was effectively lost until 1917, when his brother, Joseph Francis Daly, published *The Life of Augustin Daly,* in which Joseph included a condensed version of Augustin's account, although the biographer did reprint Collins's letter in full.[8]

At his death Charles Dickens did not leave any statement as to the intended unraveling of his plot. If we except the author's own notes for the novel, Charles Collins's testimony is the *best evidence* that ever has been, or in all likelihood ever will be, discovered concerning the fate of Edwin Drood and the guilt of John Jasper. It was written shortly after Dickens died (too soon for Collins to forget or to garble what his father-in-law had told him), there was no reason for the author to lie to his daughter's husband (on the contrary, misleading the illustrator might well have had a negative effect on the installments cover), and there was equally no reason for Collins to lie to Augustin Daly (the artist had nothing whatever to gain by providing false information to a complete stranger like Daly). Had Collins been disinclined to tell what he knew, he could, like his brother-in-law and Fildes, simply have returned a polite but meaningless reply to the playwright's inquiry, or not responded at all.

Incidentally, Augustin Daly never did write his projected adaptation of *Edwin Drood.* His own play *Divorce* became a great success around this time, and he apparently felt that Collins's information did not furnish enough detail concerning the unwritten portion of *The Mystery* to provide a satisfactory ending to the story. In this regard, it is pertinent to note that Collins in his otherwise informative letter says not a word about the critical confrontation scene at the bottom-center of the parts cover. One can only infer that Dickens did not give his illustrator the slightest hint as to what this scene was meant to represent.

The next witness to testify in print was John Forster, Dickens's longtime friend, literary executor, and biographer. In the third and final volume of his monumental *Life of Charles Dickens* (1874), Forster stated unequivocally that the story "was to be that of the murder of a nephew by his uncle," and he proceeded to provide some other details of the novel's plot that Dickens had confided to him—most significantly, in light of Fildes's later corroboration, that John Jasper's career was to end in a condemned cell.[9] Poor Forster has been attacked by the Resurrectionists ever since. Unaware of Charles Collins's earlier testimony,[10] or ignoring its implications, they have suggested that Forster was trying to pass off his own conjectures about the story-line as Dickens's confidences. Some of them even assert that the great novelist lied to his old friend about the ending of *The Mystery,* in order to ensure that the real ending would not leak out. It is true that Forster was jealously sensitive about his position with Dickens; thus if his testimony stood alone there might be some justification for questioning it. But it does not stand alone. It is confirmed by the declaration of Charles Collins, communicated privately to Augustin Daly three years before the biographer's third volume reached the public. Taken together, the statements of the two men establish that the information contributed by each independently must be the truth.

And there are three more witnesses who support Collins and Forster. Here we must consider the curiously contradictory evidence of Charles Dickens the Younger. His disappointing reply to Augustin Daly in 1870 or 1871 has already been quoted. Yet as early as 1880 Charley satisfied Joseph Hatton, with whom he collaborated on a dramatization of the novel, "that his father had revealed to him sufficient of the plot to clearly indicate how the story was to end."[11] However, Hatton failed to specify exactly what information Dickens Junior had shared with him, and he waited to publish his observations until 1905, nine years after Charley's death.

In 1891 William R. Hughes reported, "Mr. Charles Dickens informs me . . . that Edwin Drood was dead. His (Mr. Dickens's) father told him so himself."[12] And young Dickens himself wrote, in an introduction to *The Mystery* copyrighted in 1895, just a year before he died, "It was during the last walk I ever had with him at Gadshill, and our talk . . . presently drifting to *Edwin Drood,* my father asked me if I did not think he had let out too much of the story too soon. I assented, and added, 'Of course, Edwin Drood was murdered?' Whereupon he turned upon me with an expression of astonishment at my having asked such an unnecessary question, and said: 'Of course; what else do you suppose?' "[13]

If this final statement from 1895 is accurate, the only information Charley Dickens actually possessed was the fact of Edwin's murder—which, from the wording of his question to his father, he obviously considered to be self-evident. He was not told the identity of the murderer or of Dick Datchery, the means by which the culprit was to be brought to justice, or anything whatever about the conclusion of the story. In short, what little he knew he assumed most readers could figure out for themselves. No wonder he wrote to Augustin Daly "that the *Mystery of Edwin Drood* was 'as great a mystery to him as it was to the public at large.' " Only later, when the Resurrectionists began to raise their discordant voices, did Charley recognize the importance of the one crucial fact in his possession.

Luke Fildes's testimony also suffers from inconsistency, but taken as a whole it too affirms the fact of Drood's death. As we have seen, when Augustin Daly questioned Fildes in 1871 about the scenes on the parts cover, the artist revealed only that Charles Collins had rendered the cover design. Whatever else Fildes knew he kept to himself—but then Daly hadn't asked him about anything else.[14]

By February, 1884, Fildes had become more communicative. For an article published that month in *Century* magazine, he told the writer, Mrs. Alice Meynell, how he had surprised some information out of Dickens. "It happened in the following way: The artist had taken special note of a change in the description of Jasper's dress. Not only did the fact that Jasper wore in the last scenes a large black silk scarf, muffling therewith his throat and keeping his beautiful voice from cold, appear duly in the drawing, but Dickens saw that the thing had been drawn with a kind of emphasis. Mr. Fildes confessed that he had divined its significance, whereupon Dickens was somewhat troubled with the misgiving that he was telling his story too fast. The scarf was, in fact, the instrument of murder. . . .

"But finding that Mr. Fildes knew a great deal, Charles Dickens went on to make the principal revelation which concerned the central figure; he told his illustrator that Jasper was to be brought to justice in the end of the story. A drawing of this originally and most strongly conceived criminal locked up in the condemned cell (which was to have been studied at Rochester) was then planned between the two as one of the final subjects."[15]

In an interview with William R. Hughes around 1891, Fildes gave a slightly, but not materially, different version of his conversations with Dickens. According to Hughes, Fildes was "convinced that Edwin Drood should be killed by his uncle; and this opinion is supported by the fact of the introduction of a 'large black scarf of strong close-woven silk,' which Jasper wears for the first time in the fourteenth chapter of the story, and which was likely to have been the means of death; *i.e.,* by strangulation. Mr. Fildes said that Dickens seemed much surprised when he called his attention to this change of dress—very noticeable and embarrassing to an artist who had studied the character—and appeared as though he had unintentionally disclosed the secret. He further stated that it was Dickens's intention to take him to a condemned cell in Maidstone or some other gaol, in order 'that he might make a drawing,' and, said Dickens, 'do something better thanCruikshank. . . . ' "[16]

Unfortunately for Luke Fildes's credibility, in 1905 he stated as a fact what in 1891 he had expressed as his opinion. In a letter to *The Times* printed on November 3, 1905, Fildes changed the large black scarf (which *is* in the novel) to "a neckerchief of such dimensions as to go twice around the neck" (which is *not* in the book or manuscript[17]) and he quoted Dickens as saying, "Can you keep a secret? . . . I must have the double necktie! It is necessary, for Jasper strangles Edwin Drood with it."[18]

Because Fildes's memory was presumably more reliable in 1884 and 1891 than it was in 1905, it seems reasonable to infer that Charles Dickens never made the direct statement Fildes attributed to him in the latter year. Nevertheless, the illustrator was clearly given to understand that Edwin was doomed; as Fildes's son later commented, "For his part, my father was satisfied with the little he had been told by Charles Dickens—John Jasper strangled Edwin Drood and would finish up in a condemned cell—so what need was there for further argument?"[19]

Kate Dickens Collins Perugini, the author's daughter and the widow of Charles Collins, testified as a character witness for her brother Charles and for John Forster in an article written for the June 1906 issue of *Pall Mall Magazine.* While admitting that she had not received any first-hand information from her father about the resolution of his last story, she forcefully stated her conviction that it was "out of the question" for her father to mislead his lifelong friend or his son, or for either of them to distort deliberately what the author had told them.

Here is Kate's testimony in her own words: "And so [my father] told his plot to Mr. Forster, as he had been accustomed to tell his plots for years past; and those who knew him must feel it impossible to believe that in this, the last year of his life, he should suddenly become underhand, and we might say treacherous, to his old friend, by inventing for his private edification a plot that he had no intention of carrying into execution. This is incredible, and the nature of the friendship that existed between Mr. Forster and himself makes the idea unworthy of consideration. . . .

"My chief object in writing is to remind the readers of this paper that there are certain facts connected with this story that cannot lightly be put aside, and these facts are to be found in John Forster's *Life of Charles Dickens,* and in the declaration made by my brother Charles. Having known both Mr. Forster and my brother intimately, I cannot for a moment believe that either of them would speak or write that which he did not know to be strictly true; and it is on these grounds alone that I think I have a right to be heard when I insist upon the assertion that Edwin Drood was undoubtedly murdered by his uncle Jasper."[20]

At this point it is necessary to recall Charles Dickens to the witness stand. In March 1870, less than three months before his death, he made this offer to Queen Victoria (in a note to the Clerk of the Privy Council, Sir Arthur Helps): "If Her Majesty should ever be sufficiently interested in my tale to desire to know a little more of it in advance of her subjects, you know how proud I shall be to anticipate the publication."[21] If Dickens had been as fanatically determined as the Resurrectionists claim to keep his plot safe from dissemination, even to the extent of deceiving his closest friends, why did he offer to spill the beans to the one person in England whom he could not swear to secrecy? Or did he intend to lie to her too?

To sum up for the prosecution, those who believe that Drood is dead and buried can cite the evidence of Dickens's own notes and the testimony of five witnesses who enjoyed a close personal relationship with the author. Forster had long served as a kind of editorial sounding board for his friend; Collins and Fildes worked directly with Dickens to create the illustrations for the novel; young Charley, during the year or so when *Edwin Drood* was conceived and written, assisted in the production of *All the Year Round;* and Kate Dickens of all his children best understood her father.

On the other side, what evidence can the Resurrectionists cite to support their position? Only their own reading of the unfinished novel, which convinces them, in spite of all facts to the contrary, that Drood is alive and in hiding. Not one of them, as far as I have been able to discover, was personally acquainted with Dickens himself or with the five witnesses whose veracity they have tried so blithely to impugn. Not one of them, after more than a century of scholarly investigation, has dug up one scrap of tangible evidence to justify their claim that Edwin Drood "was to be one of the living characters at the close of the story."[22]

Moreover, the Resurrectionists invariably ignore, in their summing up of the evidence, the *cumulative effect* of the testimony. Rarely in a criminal case is one single piece of evidence sufficient to convict the accused person; rather it is the accumulation of facts, taken together and forming a comprehensive pattern, which leads the jury to a verdict of guilty. So with the facts in the case of *Edwin Drood.* No one of them viewed in isolation is absolutely conclusive; but in combination they prove that Charles Dickens killed his brain-child Edwin Drood.[23]

Chapter XII

Almost Perfect

Given Drood's murder, the next question to consider is, "How was he killed?" The answer will necessarily be brief, because there isn't much to say about a crime that takes place off-stage, the interest of which depends almost entirely on whether it was accomplished successfully, hardly at all on how it was done.

Both Luke Fildes and Charles Dickens the Younger expressed the belief that John Jasper strangled Edwin Drood to death.[1] Supporting this conclusion, Richard Baker lists several references to strangulation and choking in the novel,[2] and shows how Dickens managed to "Lay the ground for the manner of the murder, to come out at last" (one of the notes for Chapter 12) by having Jasper collar and choke Deputy, who "gurgles in his throat, and screws his body, and twists, as already undergoing the first agonies of strangulation." Then too, Dickens suggests the instrument as well as the method of murder, giving Jasper a large black silk scarf to wear on the eve of his nephew's disappearance.

Even more significant than any of the foregoing is the frequently quoted passage in Chapter 13 where, after Edwin decides not to tell Rosa about the engagement ring in his pocket, Dickens as narrator speaks directly—and forcefully—to the reader: "Among the mighty store of wonderful chains that are for ever forging, day and night, in the vast iron-works of time and circumstance, there was one chain forged in the moment of that small conclusion, riveted to the foundations of heaven and earth, and gifted with invincible force to hold and drag." These lines unmistakably imply that the ring was to be the primary means to John Jasper's apprehension; that all other evidence would prove inconsequential by comparison; and that therefore Jasper had committed a perfect crime *except* for Edwin's possession of this ring, about which the murderer knew nothing when he killed his nephew. In his otherwise flawless calculations, it is the "one small defect" that will bring about his destruction.

How does someone commit a "perfect" murder? The first and most essential rule is "Keep it simple." Each complication adds another possibility that something will go wrong; too many complications and something is sure to go wrong. While the choirmaster could have employed any of several methods to kill Edwin Drood, why not assume that Jasper—portrayed throughout the novel as an intelligent man—chose the very best available?

The safest, cleanest, and most efficient way for the choirmaster to dispatch Edwin is to strangle him to death in the gatehouse, after forestalling any resistance by giving him a drugged drink.[3] This modus operandi has several distinct advantages: there is virtually no chance that the assailant will fail in his attempt (Proctor and his followers notwithstanding); there is no possibility of being caught in the act by a passerby; in death by strangulation there is usually no blood or other trace of the crime, except on the victim himself; there is no "murder weapon" as such, the "large black scarf of strong close-woven silk" being returned to its everyday function immediately after the victim dies; there will be no alarm because the drug will prevent Edwin from crying out—and being indoors he would probably not be heard even if he did call for help; and once the deed is done, the killer can wait until it is quite safe to remove the body to its final destination.

Of course, even with this method Jasper does have two problems to solve. Before the murder he has to find a suitable sepulchre for his victim, and afterward he has to move the body from his rooms to this hiding place. His choice is Mrs. Sapsea's tomb, a location presenting less risk than would at first appear, because all the preparations for Drood's interment can be made *before* Jasper has to commit himself by killing Edwin. So if anything goes wrong in his preliminary arrangements—if, for example, he meets someone while depositing the quicklime in the tomb—he can always postpone the crime and alter his plans accordingly. Percy Carden has shown that Durdles's yard was in a convenient spot from which to move the lime without interference;[4] but even if Jasper were seen carrying it away, no one would suspect the purpose for which the very respectable choirmaster planned to use it.

Similarly, Jasper's successful snitching of the key to the tomb while Durdles was unconscious meant that no one could later prove he had ever had it. Whatever might be suspected about his activities on the night of the unaccountable expedition, if Jasper could "borrow" the key when Durdles was sleeping off a drunk, so in theory could anyone else, the stonemason being a notorious tippler. One further advantage to the use of Mrs. Sapsea's tomb is that those who normally had access to its key—Sapsea and Durdles—would be the first to fall under suspicion if the body were discovered there, and this red herring might impede the local police in their investigation.

As for carrying his victim's body from the gatehouse to the tomb, Jasper could go outdoors before the move and scout around to make sure no one else was prowling about. He could also bundle up the body in a blanket or bag and carry it concealed to its destination. Because no one was likely to be abroad anyway at such an hour on such a night (and Christmas Eve to boot), his chances of being apprehended during this move were almost non-existent.

No fuss, no muss, no bother—that's the way to do someone in! (Keep it in mind in case you ever need to get rid of anybody.) Yet some critics have tried to make the crime as difficult as possible for Jasper by supposing that he throws Edwin off the Cathedral tower, or down the stairwell inside the tower. This supposition is based on Jasper's opium-induced ravings to the Princess Puffer (in Chapter 23): " 'It was a journey, a difficult and dangerous journey . . . over abysses where a slip would be destruction. Look down, look down! You see what lies at the bottom there?' He has darted forward to say it, and to point at the ground, as though at some imaginary object far beneath."

Most of us interpret Jasper's "abysses" as the threat of discovery and the "slip" as a false move leading to his exposure as a murderer, while the body (which was actually at his feet) appears to be "far beneath" in his drugged state because the opium has distorted his perception of distance. But what if Jasper did decide to kill Edwin the hard way? Any plan to push his nephew off the tower presents a host of potential difficulties for which Jasper would have to be prepared: After his long walk with Neville down to the stormy river, Edwin might decline to go out again with his uncle; he might refuse to climb to the top of the tower; once up there and tumbled off, he might scream and attract attention as he fell; and worst of all, he would almost certainly create an awful mess where he hit the ground. In making his plans, Jasper would have to anticipate carrying a bloody and battered corpse to its burial place, possibly staining his clothes and leaving a trail of blood on the way, and then cleaning everything up afterward.

Come to think of it, if Jasper really hurled his nephew off the tower, why would he bother to hide the body at all? Why not just leave the bloody heap where it fell and go home to bed? After its discovery, the authorities would in all likelihood decide that Drood had fallen or jumped on his own, or that Neville was responsible for his death. The elaborate concealment of the body in quicklime is necessary to prevent the post-mortem disclosure of murder by strangulation, but it is not needed if the victim dies in a fall.

In addition to all the difficulties enumerated above, another reason for thinking that Jasper does not throw Edwin from the tower is that later he will toss Neville off that same tower. It would be neither artistic nor exciting to kill both young men in exactly the same way. But I'm getting ahead of myself—I didn't intend to dispose of Neville until my next chapter.

Chapter XIII

The First Confrontation

With the help of Durdles, Deputy, or the Opium Woman, Datchery was soon to discover Drood's body in Mrs. Sapsea's tomb. Any of the three, or all of them, could lead the detective to the hiding place: Durdles might reveal how Jasper took possession of the bundle containing the tomb key on the night of the unaccountable expedition; Deputy probably saw Jasper carrying quicklime to the tomb on that same night; and the Princess Puffer perhaps has overheard Jasper muttering something about the Sapsea monument in one of his debauches. Incidentally, Dickens must have known that quicklime would not decompose a body so entirely as to obliterate all trace of the remains, because the Mannings (whose trial and hanging he attended) buried Patrick O'Connor in quicklime and the police found O'Connor's corpse intact. Probably the author believed merely that in six months' time the corrosive would render Edwin's body unrecognizable.[1]

Having found the corpse, Datchery has still another obstacle to face, for Jasper has left no evidence in the tomb to prove that he hid the body there, let alone that he killed Edwin. Since the choirmaster has had at least six months between Drood's death and Datchery's arrival to clean up any loose ends, and since Dickens has hinted unmistakably that Grewgious's ring will be the means of Jasper's undoing,

The Preliminary Sketch (From a photograph at Dickens House)

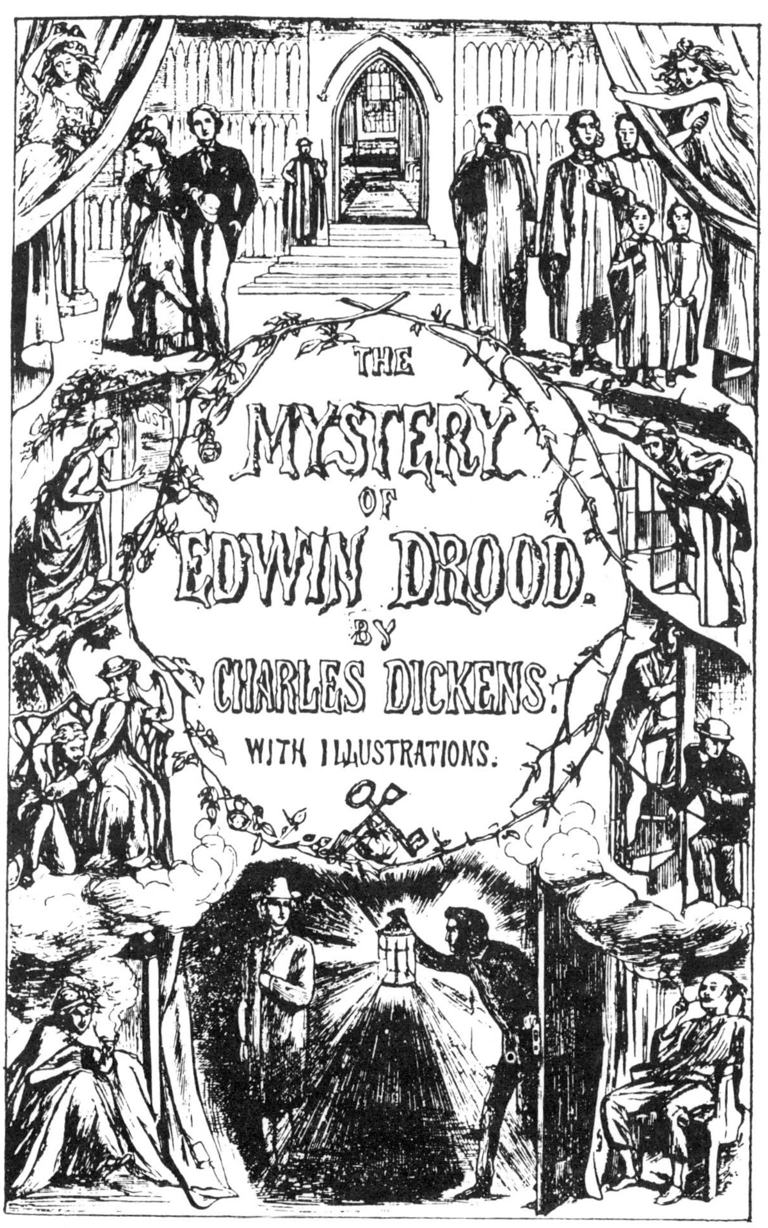

The Published Cover (Roses for Rosebud, thorns for Thornton)

there is no reason to suppose that the tomb is cluttered with clues pointing to the murderer.

Nevertheless, several commentators have placed in it some very unconvincing evidence against the choirmaster. Thus Leon Garfield,[2] Richard Proctor,[3] and others have left Jasper's scarf in the hiding place with the body—even though he had plenty of time to return and retrieve it, and no reason to leave it there in the first place. Andrew Lang makes a fuss about Edwin's coins, buttons, and keys, but even if these were found on the body and helped to identify it, they would prove only who the victim was, not who had killed him.[4] Percy Carden wants Jasper to commit a different sort of blunder; because Carden deems it aesthetically essential to bury Edwin with his forebears, he insists that Jasper has hidden the body in the Drood sarcophagus.[5] Surely Jasper has sense enough to realize that, if by some mischance the corpse were discovered in his own family vault, he himself, as the person having access to its key, would at once become the principal suspect. Similarly, the murderer would reject the Cathedral crypt, the hiding place preferred by some other critics, as too public a place to conceal a body, especially with Durdles constantly probing for "old 'uns."

So, Datchery finds the body in the Sapsea tomb but no evidence to tie the crime to John Jasper. He also finds what his employer Grewgious told him to look for particularly—the ring of diamonds and rubies delicately set in gold, still concealed on Edwin's remains. His next step is to report his discovery to Mr. Grewgious. Together they devise this plan: Jasper must be enticed to return to the tomb (to prove he knows the body is there); and someone must be waiting inside the tomb to witness his opening its door *with his own key* (to prove that he has a duplicate key and that therefore it was he who, in all probability, hid the body there in the first place).[6] Jasper must have the telltale key, because without it he would have had to leave the tomb door unlocked ever since the night of his excursion with the stonemason, when he temporarily "borrowed" Durdles's key. While the choirmaster could have afforded not to lock the door until he had actually deposited Drood's corpse there, he would hardly have risked leaving it unlocked afterward, with Durdles and Deputy and perhaps others wandering about the Cathedral precincts.

How can Jasper be inveigled into returning to the burial place? Knowing the murderer's determination to destroy Neville Landless, Datchery and Grewgious decide to tell Jasper about the ring, calculating that he will go to the tomb to recover it so that he can somehow "plant" it on Neville's person or in his lodgings. They also select Bazzard as their informant. As I pointed out in my third chapter, the clerk is one of only three persons who know about the ring, and the only one who can tell Jasper without arousing his suspicions; and besides, his making the murderer's acquaintance at Staple Inn can easily be arranged. That Bazzard is following Grewgious's instructions, not betraying him (as some critics assert), is self-evident because the allies have to know exactly *when* Jasper will arrive at the tomb, and therefore they need to know *when* Bazzard tells him the secret. Without this vital bit of information, they would have to post someone in the tomb for days or even weeks on end waiting for their quarry to show up!

Now, it must be understood that much of the information in the preceding paragraphs was not to be presented to the reader until after Jasper had gone to the tomb and fallen into the trap; perhaps even Datchery's discovery of the body would be withheld until that time. We readers have to be kept in the dark so that we as well as Jasper will experience the maximum shock when the trap is sprung. This is another reason why Bazzard is Dickens's most logical choice as the informant. Others have suggested that Jasper hears of the ring from the Princess Puffer,[7] but if she tells the secret, the astute reader is naturally going to ask, "Who told *her*?" She certainly knows nothing of the ring at the point where the story breaks off, as Edwin did not mention it in their Christmas Eve conversation. The only person who could have prompted the Opium Woman is Dick Datchery, but if the reader knows Dick set up the situation he will also know Jasper must be walking into a trap. Not much surprise there. On the other hand, if Bazzard reveals the secret, and in so doing appears to betray his employer, the reader will be left in doubt as to what will happen until Jasper actually arrives at the tomb and finds someone waiting for him.

Furthermore, and again for maximum effect, I suspect that Bazzard was to tell Jasper about the ring at the end of a monthly number. The clerk and the choirmaster have become drinking cronies—the latter hoping to make Bazzard his tool, the former playing Beckwith to Jasper's Slinkton.[8] Sitting in a tavern in their cups, Bazzard complains about the indignity of having to serve as a lawyer's clerk, and Jasper counters by grousing about his failure to find any evidence against the "murderer" Neville Landless. "Well, what about the ring?" blurts out Bazzard, accidentally on purpose. "Maybe Landless took it with him after he killed Drood."

Instantly Jasper is all ears: "What ring?" With a little prodding Bazzard soon confides the whole story to his new friend. Jasper makes some excuse and sets off at once for Cloisterham. Late that same night he goes to the tomb; unlocks the door and enters; lights his lantern; and sees, facing him in the darkness at the other side of the tomb, a dim ghost-like figure with its face obscured by the shadow of a broad-brimmed hat. Bang! The curtain falls! End of chapter, end of monthly installment!

This leaves the reader to ask himself—for a whole month, until the next installment—*Who is the figure in the tomb? Is it Drood's ghost or one of Jasper's enemies? And what is he, she, or it doing there?*

(I also toyed with the idea that the monthly number would end as Jasper inserts his key into the lock of the tomb door—that is, before he sees the figure within. But I think this alternative unlikely because of the scene on the monthly parts cover showing Jasper with lantern in hand confronting another man in a small room. This picture gives away the fact that someone or something is waiting inside the tomb, and thereby suggests that Dickens planned to have Jasper open the door and see the apparition before the installment closes.)

The next installment begins where the last ended. The ghostly figure stretches forth his left hand to reveal the ring with its rose of diamonds and rubies. "Who are you?" gasps Jasper, and the other replies in a statement to this effect: "I am Sergeant Richard Thatcher of the Detective Police; and it is my duty to place you under arrest for the murder of Edwin Drood, and to warn you that anything you say may be used in evidence at your trial."

Yes, the person waiting in the tomb is Dick Datchery, alias Sergeant Richard Thatcher (or whatever the author chose to call him). There are three reasons why this identification must be correct: first, a Scotland Yard detective would not delegate to a civilian the responsibility of facing a dangerous murderer late at night in a lonely place, and attempting to arrest him; secondly, as we shall see when we consider John Jasper's legal defense to the charge of murder, it is essential to the prosecution's case against the choirmaster that the witness who testifies to his presence at the tomb, and to his possession of a duplicate key, should be neither a friend of Neville Landless nor a dependent of Hiram Grewgious; and finally, the detective in his previous incarnation as Sergeant Dornton had a very similar experience when he waited for hours under a sofa for a thief to appear, just as Datchery waits in the tomb for John Jasper.

In fact, it may well have been this incident from "The Sofa" that suggested to Dickens the idea of Datchery's vigil in the tomb. Certainly the closing paragraphs of that story could serve, with a few minor modifications [indicated by brackets], as a dialogue between Hiram Grewgious and Sergeant Datchery. After Jasper's apprehension, the lawyer "inquired of this officer . . . whether the time appeared long, or short, when he lay [in wait] in that constrained position. . . .

" 'Why, you see, sir,' he replied, 'If . . . I had not been quite sure he was the [culprit], and would return, the time would have seemed long. But, as it was, I being dead certain of my man, the time seemed pretty short.' "

Because my identification of the figure in the tomb as a middle-aged police detective flies in the face of almost every solution previously advanced, we'll need to examine closely the two pieces of evidence that bear on this point. These are the center vignette at the bottom of the published parts cover of *Edwin Drood,* and the corresponding scene in the preliminary sketch of that cover executed by Charles Collins, the novelist's son-in-law. In both drawings, a man with a lantern, who almost everyone agrees is John Jasper, enters an unlighted room where another man apparently awaits his arrival. Who is "the Man in Wait" and where does the scene take place? I say that he's "Sergeant Datchery" and that the place is Mrs. Sapsea's tomb. There are four objections (to my knowledge) to these conclusions, three petty and one serious, but we'll consider them all.

1. Richard Baker and others object that the room in the drawing is too large to be the interior of the Sapsea tomb, and that both the door and its lock are of the wrong types for a tomb.[9] To these cavils, I reply that the artist was not told exactly what the scene was supposed to represent, nor where

it took place. To avoid disclosing too much of his story, Dickens probably provided his illustrator with only the briefest of instructions: "Draw Jasper entering a small room and being surprised to find another man already there, waiting for him."[10]

2. Baker also objects to the *open* tomb door in the drawings, pointing out that Jasper would close the door behind him before lighting his lantern, to avoid its conspicuous glare in the dark churchyard. Undoubtedly the door would be closed *in the text.* But in a single, static picture like the vignette on the cover, it would be impossible without the open door to convey the impression that Jasper had just entered the room. Presenting this same scene with the door closed and both of Jasper's hands in front of him would simply not suggest a sudden confrontation. In other words, artistic license disposes of both this and the preceding objection.

3. Andrew Lang objects that the Man in Wait wears a "paletot," or topcoat, and not a surtout like Datchery's.[11] Be honest. If you had to wait, perhaps for hours, in a tomb in a graveyard at dead of night on Christmas Eve, wouldn't you put on an overcoat if you owned one? Despite this so-called discrepancy, the man facing Jasper subtly reminds us, with his wide hat, long hair, and tightly buttoned coat, of the mysterious white-haired stranger. And this was just what Dickens wanted: a hint of Datchery but no more.

4. The only serious objection to identifying the waiting man as Sergeant Datchery is that he looks too young in the drawing on the published cover. Early theorists, who presumably did not have access to the preliminary sketch,[12] jumped to the conclusion that the figure must be a young person, like Edwin, Neville, or Helena. But the sketch creates an entirely different impression. Here the Man in Wait has a mature look—he could be any age between thirty and fifty.

Again, artistic license helps to explain the discrepancy between the textual Datchery and his portrait on the final cover. Sometime between the drawing of the original design and the execution of the later version, Dickens had decided to make his white-haired stranger clean-shaven, and stouter than he looked in Collins's first effort. Accordingly he instructed the artist in reworking the confrontation scene to remove the waiting man's mustache, and to fatten him up a bit. The net effect of these changes was to give him a much younger appearance. That this semblance of youthfulness is misleading can be seen by comparing the writer's with the artist's representation of the Opium Woman. In the text of *Edwin Drood,* the Princess Puffer is an "ugly and withered" woman "of a haggard appearance" with a "weazen chin" (Chapters 14 and 23). But a close look at the installments cover reveals an Opium Woman almost as young, buxom, and smooth-skinned as the Rosa Bud in the scenes above her! This incongruity resulted from the extremely small scale to which the vignettes were drawn. Because the artist was unable to draw wrinkles or other marks of aging effectively on his minute figures, he simply omitted them—on both the Opium Woman and Dick Datchery. And since Dickens did not want too accurate a portrayal of his detective on the parts cover, he allowed the Man in Wait to retain his deceptively youthful appearance. In fact, he probably counted on it to lead readers astray.

Perhaps this is a good place to sneak in a few incidental remarks about the installments cover. Some students of *The Mystery* believe that Charles Collins drew only the preliminary design for the cover, and that it was Luke Fildes who prepared the final version. Yet Fildes himself often denied having had anything to do with its design. Thus in 1870 or 1871 he wrote to Augustin Daly, "Mr. Charles Collins, the late Mr. Dickens' son-in-law, is the gentleman who made the design (for the cover), and in referring you to him I have no doubt you will be able to get information to your satisfaction."[13] And in a letter to S. M. Ellis dated November 29, 1914, Fildes stated, "I had better not attempt any explanation of the design of the cover of the monthly parts of 'Edwin Drood,' as it was *not* made by me. It is the work of the late Charles Collins, done before I came on the scene. . . . "[14] Whoever completed the drawing for publication, the important point is that Fildes (whether or not he touched up Collins's original) disclaimed any knowledge of what the scenes on the cover represent.

With this background information in mind, here is my elucidation (with the help of Charles Collins) of these perplexing vignettes. The flower maiden at top left represents Benevolence, Love, or just plain Goodness, and the dagger lady opposite is Malevolence, Hatred, or Evil. Next to Benevolence, Rosa Bud and Edwin Drood walk arm in arm. They have just decided to break their engagement and become "brother and sister" to each other. Across the way John Jasper with his hand to his chin watches the couple closely, trying unsuccessfully to divine the drift of their conversation. Aware of and offended by his interest, Rosa turns her head away from Jasper (*not* from Edwin), while young Drood is oblivious to this byplay, as he is in the story to Rosa's fear and loathing of his uncle. The other choristers are probably not major characters in the novel. While this scene in Chapter 13 of the text takes place *outside* the Cathedral, Dickens's notes for Part IV reveal that he originally planned to set their final interview *inside:* "Last meeting then of Rosa and Edwin in the Cathedral? *Yes.*" Later he crossed out the word "in" and wrote above it "outside." So what we have here on the cover is the scene as initially envisioned, before Dickens decided to move it outdoors.

Concerning the two scenes under Benevolence, Charles Collins tells us, "The female figure at the left of the cover reading the placard 'Lost' is only intended to illustrate the doubt entertained by Rosa Budd [*sic*] as to the fate of her lover, Drood. The group beneath it indicates the acceptance of another suitor."[15] As Charles Collins was, by Fildes's admission, the only person in the whole world (aside from Charles Dickens) who had any inside information about the identity of these characters, I see no reason to doubt his statement that both the lady at the placard and the one on the bench are Rosa Bud. Thus the only figure still to be identified here is the suitor whom Rosa accepts.

The use of the word "acceptance" suggests Tartar, as we are reasonably sure from the text that the lieutenant wins Rosa in the end. And the drawings themselves support this same conclusion. In the preliminary sketch, Drood has a small mustache, Jasper wears sideburns, and Rosa's suitor sports a beard. On the final cover, Drood is clean-shaven, Jasper retains his sidewhiskers, and the suitor has a thick handlebar mustache and either a beard or very abundant sideburns. Since Collins carefully differentiated the suitor from both Drood and Jasper *in both versions,* the differences must be intentional, and therefore the man wooing Rosa is neither Edwin nor his uncle. Her only remaining admirers are Tartar and Neville Landless, but the latter is only twenty-one when the story breaks off and neither a heavy mustache nor a full beard seems appropriate to one so young. Hence it is most likely that the suitor, as Collins implies, is Tartar. (Of course, Fildes's Tartar in the illustration "Up the River" has no beard, but the cover was prepared by a different artist long before Dickens had made up his mind about the lieutenant's appearance.)

Under the courtship scene sits the Opium Woman smoking her pipe, beyond her to the right Sergeant Datchery confronts John Jasper, and still farther to the right sprawls Jack Chinaman, the Princess Puffer's rival opium dealer.

Now we come to the three men (or four, in the preliminary sketch) climbing a narrow staircase up the right side. Here again Charles Collins provides the key to their identities: "It was intended that Jasper himself should urge on the search after Edwin Drood and the pursuit of his murderer, thus endeavoring to direct suspicion from himself, the real murderer. This is indicated in the design, on the right side of the cover, of the figures hurrying up the spiral staircase emblematical of a pursuit. They are led on by Jasper, who points unconsciously to his own figure in the drawing at the head of the title."[16]

So the man leading the chase is John Jasper. Before we try to identify the climbers below him, there is a more important question to consider. Was there to be a real, as well as an "emblematical," pursuit up the stairs of the Cathedral tower? Again siding with the majority, I believe that there was. Without Collins's information, most readers (myself included) would not guess that the pursuit was symbolic and that its leader was Jasper himself. The cover leads us to expect a chase sequence in the book, and Dickens was not the writer to disappoint us. Moreover, the text tells us that both Tartar and Crisparkle are skillful climbers, and the tower stairs and the roof of the Cathedral are excellent sites for a demonstration of their proficiency in this line.

In the emblematic chase, Collins informs us, Jasper is pointing to himself. But at whom does he point in the actual chase? From the time of Drood's disappearance, Jasper has pursued Neville while the forces of justice have stalked Jasper. What could be more fitting than to encapsulate this drama of persecution and retribution in the pursuit up the tower stairs?

In other words, Neville Landless, who is not shown in the drawings, has preceded Jasper up the staircase, and it is at *Neville* that the murderer points!

As for the two men below Jasper on the final cover, they must be Tartar and Crisparkle. Considered together, the two versions of the cover strongly support this identification. Because it was the author's original intention to have Sergeant Datchery call in the local police to help him arrest John Jasper, the preliminary design shows three policemen chasing the choirmaster. Once Dickens had conceived the characters of the sturdy sailor Tartar and the manly Christian Crisparkle, he decided to give them a chance to display their mettle by capturing Jasper, and so he had Collins substitute the two heroes for the three constables. In the drawing, "Tartar's" face is hidden behind the post (perhaps so he will not be recognized as Rosa's beau across the way), but otherwise he looks not unlike her suitor—at least he seems to be clothed in the same style. As for the man lowest on the stairs, there has been considerable disagreement as to whether or not he is dressed in clerical garb, but he wears a dark jacket and no necktie, and the white splotch under his sideburns looks to me like a feeble attempt to depict a clergyman's collar. Accordingly I have always seen in the third man a hazy portrait of the Reverend Mr. Crisparkle.

Finally, note the heavy line separating Jasper from the policemen in the preliminary sketch, which clearly divides the chase sequence into two distinct scenes. I think this break was meant to suggest an interval of some distance between Jasper and his pursuers; he was not just a few steps above them as he seems to be in the final version.

Now, back to the story. After Datchery tells Jasper he is under arrest, the choirmaster turns and flees. But the detective has anticipated Jasper's attempt to escape—hiding in strategic locations around the Cathedral grounds are Tartar, Crisparkle,

Neville, and possibly others. Datchery, who had earlier obtained from Durdles the keys for the Cathedral doors as well as for the Sapsea tomb, has stationed Neville in what he considers a safe place—at the summit of the Cathedral tower, where Landless is instructed to act as a lookout. To allow the youth to come and go as necessary, Dick unlocks the main door of the Cathedral and the iron gate to the tower, and leaves these entryways unlocked.

But Datchery has miscalculated, for Jasper, finding the other paths blocked, heads toward the Cathedral. Seeing him approach, young Landless shouts out something like, "He's coming past the Cathedral entrance! Get him!" Jasper hears his cry, looks up and sees him leaning over the parapet. The murderer determines to destroy Neville before he himself is captured, and thus fulfill his "second object" in life. He enters the Cathedral through the main door and proceeds to the iron gate leading to the tower stairs (both of which he finds unlocked). Working himself into a fury at the thought of his enemies' trap and Neville's triumph, he races up the tower staircase!

Far below, Tartar and Crisparkle struggle to catch up with him, while Datchery, puffing and panting and "reddening with the exertion," brings up the rear. At the summit, Jasper finds Neville waiting for him. Bravely the younger man throws himself upon his adversary, but he is no match for the maddened murderer. Jasper lifts him like a child from his feet and hurls him from the tower! With a terrible scream (the fulfillment of Durdles's prophetic ghost shriek) Neville falls to his death. Tartar and Crisparkle, after some heroic clambering around the roof of the Cathedral, overcome the choirmaster and bring him back to the waiting Datchery.

With Jasper's wrist securely handcuffed to his own, the detective directs the removal of Edwin's body from its bed of quicklime, and of Neville's from the base of the Cathedral

Death Plunge

tower. Side by side, the remains of the two young men are temporarily interred in the Sapsea tomb, or perhaps in the Drood family sarcophagus (conveniently located in the same graveyard), safe from the curious gaze of passers-by. Thus the enigmatic question heading Chapter 14, "When Shall These Three Meet Again?" was to be answered, as it is in *Macbeth,* "When the hurlyburly's done, / When the battle's lost and won." Lost because Neville has died in the struggle, won because John Jasper has been exposed and captured.

After completing this task, Datchery and the others, now joined by Mr. Grewgious, bring Jasper before a magistrate and accuse him of Edwin's murder. Given Dickens's sense of irony, I suspect that this magistrate was to be none other than our old friend, Mayor Sapsea. As Grewgious explains to the mayor why Jasper should be placed in custody, Dickens—using the lawyer as his mouthpiece—now reveals to the reader all the details of the plan to trap the murderer. Because Jasper stubbornly refuses to speak, or reserves his defense, or both, Sapsea has no choice but to order that he be held for trial, and the chapter ends.[17]

At last Jasper has been arrested for his crime—but can he be convicted?

Chapter XIV

John Jasper's Defense

> The duty of counsel for the prosecution is simply to present the facts: those that tell in favour of the prisoner equally with those that tell against him. He is not to press for a conviction or to influence the jury by rhetoric or appeals to prejudice. . . . But counsel for the defence may do almost anything he likes. He may gloss over any of the facts which appear awkward; he may introduce all kinds of irrelevant matter to confuse the issue; he may appeal to the most sacred emotions of the jury or to their shabbiest prejudices.
>
> —C. P. Harvey, Q. C.[1]

It is impossible to tell from the existing *Drood* fragment whether Dickens planned to devote several chapters, or just a few brief paragraphs, to John Jasper's trial for the murder of Edwin Drood. Nevertheless, the outcome of the trial is a crucial event in the story. If Jasper is guilty, as most readers believe, he must be convicted and punished for his crime. To convict him, the prosecution must develop convincing evidence of his guilt, and find credible witnesses to present this evidence to the jury. Equally important is the consideration that John Jasper was to be tried in an English court under English law, and that therefore all the applicable English rules of evidence and procedure would have had to be followed for the prosecution to secure a conviction.

Scene from the Trial of John Thurtell

Many of those who have written about *The Mystery of Edwin Drood* have overlooked these obvious truths. They have convicted Jasper without evidence; failed to consider the inadequacies of their witnesses; and violated due process and the rights of the accused a dozen times over. The writer who best exemplifies this flouting of the rules of English jurisprudence is Edwin Charles. In his *Keys to the Drood Mystery,* Charles has his protagonists, two of whom are Scotland Yard officers, follow Jasper to an opium den and extract a confession from him while he's under the influence of the drug.[2] Such a confession would be worthless—no English judge of any competence or integrity would admit it into evidence; and Richard Mayne, joint Commissioner of the Metropolitan Police at the time the story is set, and a barrister by training, would have severely reprimanded any of his men who employed such unethical methods.[3]

My scenario for Jasper's trial (which follows) attempts to avoid these shortcomings. On the other hand, it is based on the unverifiable assumption that the choirmaster will do what any reasonably prudent murderer would do in his situation: hire the best lawyers that money can buy and fight the charges against him with every weapon he can find.[4]

Regardless of Datchery's identity or Drood's death or survival, Jasper has a perfectly viable defense that would apply to any solution of the mystery in which he is brought to trial. This defense consists of three main lines of argument:

1. Jasper will flatly deny that he murdered, or attempted to murder, his nephew Edwin Drood.

2. He will assert that Hiram Grewgious and Neville Landless are the leaders of a criminal conspiracy against him, and that they and their cohorts have falsely and maliciously combined to convict him of a crime of which he is entirely innocent. I don't mean to imply that Jasper's advocates will *formally* accuse the choirmaster's enemies of conspiracy,

only that they will put the jury on notice that Grewgious and the others were determined to prosecute their client by any means, fair or foul, and that conspiring in this way constitutes a crime.[5]

3. Jasper will claim that the death of Neville Landless was accidental, or that he killed Neville in self-defense. In either case, the moral responsibility for Neville's death, according to Jasper and his lawyers, rests with Grewgious and the other conspirators and *not* with the choirmaster. "If they had not persecuted our client, Mr. John Jasper, Neville Landless would still be alive today!"

Now let's see how this defense applies to one of the oldest theories about *Edwin Drood,* promulgated in 1887 by Richard A. Proctor in his famous book, *Watched by the Dead.* In Proctor's solution, Edwin is alive and it is he who assumes the role of Dick Datchery and returns to Cloisterham to spy on his uncle; Drood and Grewgious have joined forces to "punish" Jasper for his attempt on Edwin's life; Edwin as Datchery confronts Jasper in the Sapsea tomb; Neville struggles with Jasper on the Cathedral tower and "receives his death-wound";[6] and Jasper is tried and convicted for the murder of *Neville,* not Edwin.

Proctor obviously gave little thought to Jasper's trial. If Drood is alive, there is not a shred of evidence that it was Jasper who attacked him, or in fact that the alleged attack took place at all. There were no witnesses to the crime, save for Edwin and Jasper themselves, and the uncle's word is as good as or better than his nephew's. Remember, Jasper can call such excellent witnesses to his good character as Mr. Thomas Sapsea, the Mayor of Cloisterham; the Dean of Cloisterham Cathedral; the verger Mr. Tope and his wife; and even (to embarrass the choirmaster's enemies) the Reverend Septimus Crisparkle, who would have no choice but to admit under oath that Jasper bore a spotless reputation in Cloisterham.

Jasper's lawyers would mount a strong counterattack with their conspiracy theory. Hiram Grewgious, a vindictive old busybody, for obscure reasons has long borne an implacable enmity toward Jasper; Grewgious has persuaded the gullible Crisparkle and the others that Jasper tried to kill Drood; and he has gained such an ascendancy over Edwin's mind that the young weakling has been prevailed upon to allege an assault that never really occurred—or if it did, it was Neville Landless or some unknown third party who committed it.

As for Neville's death, the conspirators and not Jasper are clearly responsible for that calamity. Why, when they had *no proof whatever* of Jasper's supposed attack on Edwin, did they maliciously set a trap for the choirmaster in the empty tomb? Through his counsel Jasper would assert that he did not intend to kill Neville, but in the struggle on the tower he pushed Neville away and over he went. (The tower's parapet must be quite low, as Durdles in a "mild fit of calenture . . . would as lief walk off the tower into the air as not" *ED,* Chapter 12.) How can the prosecution *prove* that Jasper's shove was murder and not self-defense? Neville had no right to harass and pursue Jasper in the first place, since Jasper to that point had committed no crime.

Under cross-examination Edwin Drood (who is not clever out of his own line) will make a particularly pathetic witness. How can he explain why he waited a full year to accuse his uncle of attacking him? Why did Edwin allow Neville Landless to suffer under the suspicion of murder all that time when he knew from the beginning that Neville was innocent? If there was an attack on Drood, wasn't Neville's death the direct result of Edwin's failure to speak out at once?

Jasper, denying that he ever had in his possession a key to the Sapsea tomb, will declare that he saw the tomb door open (or saw the key in its lock) and decided to investigate. How can Edwin prove that his uncle had his own key? Without a body, the presence of quicklime in the tomb means nothing, because anyone could have put the stuff there. For every point raised by the prosecution, the defense can show either that (like the quicklime) it is immaterial, or that (like the key) it boils down to Edwin's word against Jasper's—and what hard-headed British jury would believe someone stupid enough to wait a year before making an accusation of attempted murder?

As this brief outline shows, Proctor's solution is untenable because there is no way that a fair-minded jury would find the choirmaster guilty of any of the charges against him. This same conclusion also holds true for all the other theories in which Edwin survives, but someone else is Dick Datchery. If his nephew is not dead, there is no crime for which Jasper can be convicted because there is no proof, and under English law the accused is presumed to be innocent until he is *proved* guilty. If Jasper is not convicted, his career cannot end in the condemned cell, as Dickens told Forster, and hinted to Fildes, that it would. With or without the condemned cell, how can the story have a satisfactory conclusion if no crime can be brought home to the perpetrator?

So much for Richard Proctor and his school. Most other theorists believe that Drood is dead, and that Dick Datchery is one of the following: Neville, Helena, Grewgious, Bazzard, or Tartar. Because in these solutions the prosecution can produce Edwin's murdered body, Jasper's advocates have to take a somewhat different tack. To win an acquittal for their client, his lawyers must shift the blame from Jasper to someone else; and they have a prime suspect conveniently at hand in the person of Neville Landless. This is a plausible line of defense because Neville as well as Jasper had both motive and opportunity to commit the crime. If there's a reasonable doubt as to which of the two is guilty, the benefit of that doubt goes to the prisoner, and the jury must—or at least should—acquit him.

With Drood dead, the choirmaster's lawyers would still try to convince the jury of the existence of a criminal conspiracy against their client, in order to discredit the testimony of the prosecution's key witnesses. The principal witness, of course, is the person who faced Jasper in the Sapsea tomb; the case for the prosecution turns on the evidence of this witness. While other enemies of Jasper were hidden on that fateful night somewhere in the vicinity of the graveyard, they could hardly have been stationed close enough (without his seeing them) to swear that he opened the tomb door with his own key. Only the person inside could testify to that fact. How would the defense challenge each of those characters whom other critics nominate to confront the choirmaster?

If it was Neville Landless in the tomb, his testimony is of no value whatever to the prosecution. Because he is himself a major suspect, anything he says can be construed as an attempt to conceal his own guilt. The jury would be much more likely to believe the level-headed, respectable choirmaster than they would someone like Neville Landless, by repute "a dangerously passionate fellow, of an uncontrollable and furious temper" and a "vindictive and violent nature" (*ED,* Chapters 10 and 16).

As for Helena Landless, the defense need only point out that Neville's sister would do anything necessary to vindicate her brother—someone of her bold and self-possessed character would not stick at a lie to save him from disgrace. Helena's very presence in the tomb would invalidate her testimony. What was a nice young Victorian lady doing in a place like that anyway? Anyone capable of this kind of impropriety would certainly be capable of perjuring herself for Neville's sake.

Even those who believe Datchery is Hiram Grewgious do not have the effrontery to suggest it was the old lawyer who faced Jasper that night. Had he been foolish enough to do so, the virile young choirmaster would no doubt have broken his neck. For the sake of argument, however, let's put him in the tomb. As the leader of Jasper's persecutors, Grewgious would be particularly susceptible to attack, especially if the defense managed to draw out of Crisparkle an admission that the lawyer had referred to the eminently respectable choirmaster—*before* there was any evidence against him—as a slinking individual, a brigand, and a wild beast. The old man's animosity could be represented to the jury as pure spiteful malice, and as such would lend support to the argument that he had fomented a criminal conspiracy against the accused.

Bazzard is another poor choice for the figure in the tomb. As Grewgious's employee—the defense would uncharitably call him Grewgious's tool—he could easily be accused of testifying to anything his employer wanted him to say.

Of all the "Staple Inn Alliance," Tartar would make the best witness, since he is independently wealthy and least subject to the influence of either Neville or Grewgious. On the other hand, Jasper's counsel could point out Tartar's close personal ties to Rosa Bud and Septimus Crisparkle, two of Neville's staunchest supporters. The defense might also describe Tartar, a private citizen with no direct involvement in the case, as a meddling idler with nothing better to do than persecute their client.

To sum up, one important fact has been overlooked by all previous commentators. At Jasper's trial "the Man in Wait" ought to make a good witness for the prosecution; yet most of those so far considered would under cross-examination make better witnesses for the defense!

What sort of witness would Sergeant Datchery of the Metropolitan Police have made, if it was he who confronted Jasper in the tomb? In 1843, when the detective arrested Jasper, the force administered by Colonel Charles Rowan and Mr. Richard Mayne had been in existence for some fourteen years. By this time it had established a reputation for integrity unrivaled in English, or in fact European, police history—a reputation that remained untarnished until several years after the novelist's death.[7] Thus the testimony of a Metropolitan Police officer would have been received with great respect by both judge and jury. This was especially so in 1844 (the year of Jasper's trial) when Scotland Yard's arrest and conviction of François Courvoisier for the murder of Lord William Russell (1840) were still fresh in everyone's mind.

Even though Grewgious would have paid the sergeant's expenses in Cloisterham (as was the custom of the day), he could have exercised no direct control over the detective in the performance of his duty. Datchery was answerable only to his superiors at Scotland Yard—meaning, ultimately, to Commissioners Rowan and Mayne—and to no one else. As an independent witness, the policeman's testimony would necessarily carry much greater weight than that of Grewgious's dependents or Neville's friends.

Of course, most of the characters mentioned above were to bear witness against Jasper. Grewgious would tell how he became suspicious of the choirmaster after Edwin's disappearance, and how he employed Sergeant Datchery to investigate; Rosa's testimony would establish Jasper's motive; Durdles, Deputy, and perhaps the Opium Woman would add their links to the chain of evidence (though I'm not at all sure the prosecution would actually call the Princess Puffer—she'd look so scruffy and disreputable on the witness stand!); and Bazzard would testify how he told Jasper the secret of the engagement ring, and how the choirmaster at once set off for Cloisterham to retrieve it.

But the truly vital testimony is Sergeant Datchery's: how he found Drood's body with the help of Durdles and Deputy; how he borrowed the keys to the Sapsea tomb and the Cathedral from the stonemason; how he was locked in the tomb by Tartar and Crisparkle (better witnesses than most); how he waited there in the darkness for several hours until Jasper at last arrived and opened the door with his duplicate key; how Jasper lighted his lamp and discovered the detective waiting for him; and finally, when the sergeant told him he was under arrest, how Jasper turned and fled from the tomb. It is this evidence which proves that Jasper knew where the body was hidden, and that (in possessing his own key) he was most likely to be the one who had put it there. Perhaps Datchery, with the resources of Scotland Yard behind him, would also have been able to find the locksmith who made Jasper's duplicate key.[8] (The conspicuous presence of this key on the cover of the monthly installments probably means that it was destined to play a significant part in the story.)

During cross-examination Jasper's lawyers would do their best to shake the detective's statement that Jasper entered the tomb with his own key, just as they would if Datchery were any other character, but it is incontrovertible that the testimony of a Scotland Yard officer on this point would be infinitely more convincing than that of anyone else.

Because Datchery's evidence clinches the case against Jasper, the jury returns a verdict of guilty as charged. But the story does not end here, because even now Jasper is not ready to concede defeat.

Chapter XV

The Second Confrontation

Thanks to Sergeant Datchery's testimony, John Jasper is convicted of Edwin Drood's murder, but he still refuses to confess. After all, why should he? Undoubtedly Jasper has many sympathizers—people like Sapsea and Honeythunder—who remain convinced that the choirmaster is innocent and Neville Landless is guilty. To concede that Jasper is the murderer would be to admit that they were wrong about Jasper and Neville from the beginning, and types like the mayor and the philanthropist would hardly relish such an admission. Perhaps a number of these "croakers," whom Dickens in his later years had come to despise, would have tried to get Jasper a commutation of his death sentence, or even a pardon—as some well-wishers managed to do for the alleged murderer Thomas Smethurst, much to Dickens's disgust.[1]

So long as Jasper denies his guilt, there will be an imperishable blight on Neville's good name. How can the real murderer be persuaded or even compelled to confess, and thus vindicate young Landless? Aubrey Boyd, in an article published in October 1921, was first to suggest the means of wringing a confession from the choirmaster. After reviewing the many references in *Edwin Drood* to "animal magnetism," or mesmerism, Boyd ventured the brilliant conjecture that "Datchery should gather evidence that would carry the pursuit of the criminal forward until an impasse was reached, which Helena, by her remarkable gift [of hypnotic power], would transcend." Stated in more practical terms, Datchery manages to secure Jasper's conviction in a court of law, but the detective is not able to break his antagonist's spirit—even after his conviction Jasper remains unrepentant and defiant. Something more is needed, and Helena alone has the power to shatter the villain's resistance. Boyd went on to suggest vaguely how this was to be accomplished: "the circumstances of Jasper's crime were to be 'elicited from him as if told of another' by means of the telepathic principle to which Helena held a key."[2] Unfortunately, Boyd said nothing more specific about the way Helena would have gained the desired end. Was she to extract the confession from a distance, by some form of mental telepathy? Or was she somehow to enter Jasper's cell and confront her enemy?

In *The Drood Murder Case* (1951), Richard M. Baker opts for the latter alternative, and accordingly deserves credit for being the first to publish (what I consider to be) the correct conclusion of the mystery. Helena, he says, "was to confront Jasper in the likeness of her twin brother, dressed in his clothes, in a scene of great import" set in the murderer's condemned cell, "and there she would force him by means of her mesmeric power to confess the details of Edwin's murder."[3] This dramatic encounter was something of an afterthought on Baker's part, and he does not explain *why* it is necessary for Helena to wrest a confession from Jasper; but I am sure the reasons are Jasper's obstinate refusal to confess, and Helena's determination to clear her brother of all suspicion.

This climax fits in extraordinarily well with hints in the novel itself, with incidents in certain other stories by Dickens, and with John Forster's statement about the ending of *The Mystery.* Helena's exploits as a child, when "she dressed as a boy, and showed the daring of a man," clearly foreshadow a later situation when she was again to disguise herself as a man. Just as clearly, this man was not to be the genial, middle-aged Datchery, whom she does not resemble at all, but rather her own twin brother, to whom she bears a very striking likeness. Helena is as tall, or almost as tall, as Neville, as we see in Fildes's illustrations and in Rosa's description of herself as "a mite of a thing" compared to "such a noble creature" as Helena (*ED,* Chapter 7). And Joe the coachman remarks of Neville, "His is the build of a girl to mine" (Chapter 15). So brother and sister are similar in height and physique as well as in features, coloring, and manner (Chapter 6).

The real question then is not *whether* Helena will disguise herself as Neville, but *when* she will do so. As there is no need to assume his identity so long as he can act for himself, it follows that she was to pass for her twin only *after* he had been disabled or killed. Nevertheless, most writers place her stint in male attire and her confrontation with Jasper *before* her brother's death and *before* the murderer's arrest. Percy Carden, for example, has Helena dressed in Neville's clothes (but pretending to be Edwin!) facing Jasper in the Drood family sarcophagus, and being all but fatally strangled by the murderer.[4] Such a development is doubtful because neither Crisparkle nor Grewgious would have allowed Helena to face a desperate killer alone in a deserted place.

Richard Baker, on the other hand, after speculating that Helena would confront Jasper before the tomb scene,[5] changed his mind and moved the decisive encounter to the condemned cell after Jasper's trial. It was the evidence of John Forster that led Baker to revise his solution. In Forster's account of what Dickens told him about the novel's ending, the biographer states, "the originality of [the story] was to consist in the review of the murderer's career by himself at the close, when its temptations were to be dwelt upon as if, not he the culprit, but some other man, were the tempted.

The last chapters were to be written in the condemned cell, to which his wickedness, all elaborately elicited from him as if told of another, had brought him."[6]

If we accept this statement as the unadulterated truth (as I do), then it is manifest that Jasper's confession was to bear some very important relationship to the plot or theme of the novel as a whole. Yet at first glance there seems to be nothing very original or significant about a confession at the end of a murderer's career, or even about his narrating it in the third person. In fact, such a confession, if carried over more than one chapter, as Forster's statement implies, could become intolerably boring. How did Dickens plan to sustain reader interest during Jasper's lengthy discourse? And Forster's synopsis raises several other questions. Why does Jasper confess as if of another? Why does his confession have to be elaborately elicited? And *who* elicits the confession?

Everything falls into place if we imagine the following scene in John Jasper's prison cell. The condemned man sits at a table at the rear of the cell. The jailer enters and tells Jasper that Mr. Tope, the verger of Cloisterham Cathedral, has come to visit him. Will he see Tope? Jasper consents; exit the jailer. A man enters the cell and the door clangs shut behind him. The visitor approaches the table and Jasper looks up into his face. The choirmaster is literally petrified with amazement as he recognizes the features of Neville Landless—*a man he knows is dead!* There follows a battle of wills between the newcomer and the prisoner, but so shocked is Jasper that the visitor's mind gradually achieves dominance over the murderer's. Now with the power of mesmeric influence "Neville" forces Jasper to confess. Because he is in a kind of trance, Jasper relates his confession as if another man had committed his crimes. In the struggle of wills between "Neville" and Jasper, the latter's narrative has to be dragged out of him—elaborately elicited—word by word. At last the murderer signs a statement admitting his guilt and absolving Neville, and his ghostly visitor leaves.

Because Helena's confrontation of Jasper would have much greater impact if it at first appeared that the visitor was truly a ghost, only *after* the scene ended would Dickens have revealed that Jasper's nemesis was not Neville's spirit but Helena in disguise. The author's more devoted readers would have recognized in this spectral visitation similarities to situations in two short stories he published in the same decade as *Edwin Drood:* "The Portrait Painter's Story" (1861), in which the ghost of a recently deceased woman encounters the artist who has been commissioned to paint her portrait; and "The Trial for Murder" (1865), in which a murdered man's ghost appears to the foreman of the accused murderer's jury.[7]

A few details concerning Helena's preparations for her meeting with the condemned man may help to clarify the reasoning behind my outline of events. For one thing, why should she identify herself as Mr. Tope? By posing as Jasper's landlord (a man with whom the jailers would presumably not be acquainted), Helena could get inside the cell without putting Jasper on his guard, and without having to disclose her intentions to the prison authorities, who might take a dim view of her plan to trick Jasper into a confession. As I envision the situation, Helena (already disguised as a man) and Septimus Crisparkle come to the jail together. When they meet the prison officials, Crisparkle does almost all the talking. Mr. Tope, he explains, is a good friend of the prisoner; Tope wishes to speak with Jasper in the hope of inducing him to tell the truth about Drood's slaying. While Helena is in the cell with the murderer, Crisparkle and one of the guards wait outside (where Jasper cannot see them), ready to rush in if needed.

The second point is more basic. How does Helena persuade Mr. Crisparkle to assist her in the scheme to make

Jasper talk? Of course Crisparkle loves her, but this fact alone would not influence a man of principle like the minor canon. Rather Helena convinces him he has a moral obligation to help exonerate her innocent brother; moreover, she confides that the idea of impersonating the dead man originated with Neville himself—for the "complete understanding" between the twins continues beyond the grave. Nothing like a soupçon of the supernatural (à la *The Moonstone*) to spice up a mystery story.[8]

But the conscientious cleric, whose first duty, in his own words, "is towards those who are in necessity and tribulation," has an even more urgent reason for cooperating with Helena. By now he has become convinced that Jasper really did murder Edwin. The minor canon has spoken to Jasper since his conviction, perhaps more than once, and has tried unsuccessfully to persuade him to confess. As Crisparkle realizes, Jasper in his efforts to save his miserable life is risking his immortal soul. There is no hope of his salvation until he confesses his crime. And so Crisparkle complies with Helena's proposal as the only way to rescue Jasper from eternal damnation.

It may be objected that extracting a confession in this way would violate Jasper's civil rights. Not so. Under English criminal law during Dickens's lifetime, a *convicted* murderer had no rights. There was at that time no appeals process and the sentence of the trial judge was final. Well, almost final. It was possible for the Home Secretary to commute the sentence of death to a term of imprisonment, or even to grant a pardon (as Jasper and his supporters hoped would happen in his case). But the Home Secretary very rarely intervened in this way.

According to John Forster, Dickens remarked, when he was first planning the novel, that he had "a very curious and new idea for my new story. Not a communicable idea (or the interest of the book would be gone) but a very strong one, though difficult to work."[9] What Dickens had in mind as his new but difficult-to-work idea has aroused endless speculation. In my opinion, most of the explanations adduced to account for these provocative phrases either have contained nothing new (that is, nothing original) or have not been particularly hard to work. Bringing Edwin Drood back to life would certainly not have been a new idea: Mary Elizabeth Braddon, Thomas Speight, and Dickens himself had already resurrected the supposedly dead several times in the decade preceding *Drood.* The disclosure of Dick Datchery's identity, whoever he really is, would not constitute a new or difficult-to-work feature, as Aubrey Boyd forcefully argues: "Nothing surely was less new in the fiction of [Dickens's] time than the avenger incognito. The most unexpected identification at the end could not make it an extraordinary story element—not even the grotesque revelation . . . of Helena Landless as Datchery."[10] More compelling is Montagu Saunders's contention that the new idea had to do with Jasper's unconsciously fastening the noose around his own neck when he devoted himself to Neville's destruction.[11] But while the choirmaster's unwitting self-pursuit would certainly have proved of great significance in the novel's development, it does not seem especially hard to work, nor was it entirely original. Lady Lytton's *Cheveley* (1839) employs a similar plot device, the villainous Lord De Clifford ruining himself when his scheme to convict and transport an innocent man backfires.[12]

Like Richard Baker, therefore, I maintain that the new but difficult-to-work idea involved Helena's appearance as the shade of Neville in Jasper's condemned cell. This concept is certainly original; I know of no earlier Victorian mystery story where a bogus ghost forces a murderer to confess;[13] and it was decidedly difficult to effectuate because Dickens needed to manipulate the reader's emotions without losing that willing suspension of disbelief on which the success of his novel depended. First he would have had to convey the impression that Jasper was being challenged by a "real" ghost; then, after the confession had been obtained and Helena's impersonation revealed, to win our acceptance of this dazzling twist in the plot. As Dickens himself observed, when he praised Wilkie Collins's *Moonstone* by saying it had "nothing belonging to disguised women or the like,"[14] it is not an easy task to disguise a woman convincingly as a man; it is even more difficult to represent her as a man's ghost, capable of hoodwinking someone as cunning and wary as John Jasper; and it is most difficult, after creating such an illusion, to reveal it was all a hoax without alienating one's readers.

Another statement by John Forster has elicited much scorn from the Resurrectionists. After quoting Dickens as saying that his "very curious and new idea" was "Not a communicable idea (or the interest of the book would be gone)," Forster at once adds in his own words, "The story, as I learnt immediately afterward, was to be that of the murder of a nephew by his uncle. . . . "[15] Why, ask Proctor and his disciples, did Dickens reveal his story "immediately" if his doing so would destroy the interest of the book? The answer, of course, is that Dickens confided to others only what he considered unimportant—that Drood was done in by Jasper—but he did not tell Forster, his son, his illustrators, or anyone else about the remarkable series of developments on which he actually intended the interest of the work to depend. These include Jasper's discovery of the grim figure waiting for him in Drood's burial place; Dick Datchery's triumphant revelation of his true identity;[16] the pursuit up the tower stairs and the death of Landless; and most electrifying of all, "Neville's" return from the grave to face his enemy and break his spirit.

Chapter XVI

Object Lesson

We've seen how Dickens planned the circumstances surrounding John Jasper's confession to generate as much excitement as possible. But what did he have in mind for the confession itself? To justify his confidence to Forster concerning its importance, Dickens needed to throw in some surprises to enliven the killer's lengthy soliloquy. I suspect one of them would have been the revelation that the music-master's frenzied passion for Rosa Bud concealed a more profound motive for the crime.

True, Jasper's purpose at first glance seems to be beyond dispute: he wants to put his nephew out of the way so he can possess Edwin's fiancée for himself. Yet the "wonderfully childish, wonderfully whimsical" Rosa is hardly the sort of woman one would expect the sombre choirmaster to kill for; and there is no guarantee she will accept him after he has disposed of his unsuspecting rival. As Rosa herself reflects (in Chapter 20), " 'What motive could he have, according to my accusation?' She was ashamed to answer in her mind, 'The motive of gaining me!' And covered her face, as if the lightest shadow of the idea of founding murder on such an idle vanity were a crime almost as great."

If Rosa is right in regarding Jasper's infatuation as insufficient grounds for homicide, then what really motivated the

The Night Previous to Execution

choirmaster? Like Rodion Raskolnikov, John Jasper is a man who has something to prove, and murder is the means he employs to prove it. What he hopes to do is convince himself that his existence is not a meaningless nullity, as he fears it may be. Of his life in Cloisterham, the choirmaster admits to Edwin, "I hate it. The cramped monotony of my existence grinds me away by the grain. How does our service sound to you?"

"Beautiful! Quite celestial!"

"It often sounds to me quite devilish. I am so weary of it. The echoes of my own voice among the arches seem to mock me with my daily drudging round. No wretched monk who droned his life away in that gloomy place, before me, can have been more tired of it than I am. He could take for relief (and did take) to carving demons out of the stalls and seats and desks. What shall I do? Must I take to carving them out of my heart?"

These are not the words of a man obsessed by love. Nor does Jasper need to carve demons out of his heart, for he has already found a more satisfactory way to relieve his anguish: nothing less than the plotting of a flawless murder. By violating the most sacred law of God and man—"Thou shalt not kill"—he will rise above the narrow constraints of his life as "a poor monotonous chorister and grinder of music" and find suitable scope for his restless but ill-defined ambitions and aspirations. As he works out the details of his scheme to strangle his nephew, murder becomes not just a means to gain Rosa Bud, but a new, stimulating, and meaningful *object in life.*

"One object in life"! Variations of this phrase turn up again and again throughout the mystery. It appears initially as one of the contemplated titles on the first page of Dickens's notes for the novel, and again in the notes as a comment upon Chapter 15: "Jasper's failure in the one great object made known by Mr. Grewgious." Note that this remark makes no sense if Rosa herself is "the one great object." At this point Drood had already been dispatched, and the way to the lady stood open. So why was the crime a failure? Because Jasper saw the murder as an act capable of giving meaning to "his past and his present wasted life"; and Grewgious has revealed to him that the deed was meaningless after all.

The pregnant phrase crops up again in Chapter 5 of the novel itself, where Durdles applies it to Deputy's job of stoning the mason home every night. "Own brother, sir, . . . to Peter the Wild Boy! But I gave him an object in life."

"At which he takes aim?" Mr. Jasper suggests.

"That's it, sir," returns Durdles, quite satisfied; "at which he takes aim. I took him in hand and gave him an object. What was he before? A destroyer. What work did he do? Nothing but destruction."

Whereas Deputy's object in life turns him from destructive to constructive behavior, Jasper's takes him the other way, from his constructive chores as the respected Lay Precentor and choirmaster of Cloisterham Cathedral to the destructive business of homicide. First he murders Edwin, and then, instead of devoting full time to the pursuit of the supposedly irresistible Rosebud, he discovers "a second object that has arisen in my life": the destruction of Neville Landless.

Even before Drood's murder, Jasper has marked Neville for death. Just as Deputy takes aim at *his* object in life, so Jasper "watches Neville, as though his eye were at the trigger of a loaded rifle, and he had covered him, and were going to fire. A sense of destructive power is so expressed in his face, that even Durdles pauses in his munching, and looks at him, with an unmunched something in his cheek" (Chapter 12).

Although Rosa supplies the ostensible reason for the choice of Neville Landless as his second object in life, once again she is merely an excuse for action. "If you really suppose," Rosa pleads with him, "that I favour Mr. Landless, or that Mr. Landless has ever in any way addressed himself to me, you are wrong." Even though Jasper must recognize the truth of her assertion, he does not pause in his persecution of the hapless youngster. Like a tiger who has tasted human blood, he has become addicted, and to satisfy his craving he is compelled to claim another victim.

Compared to the thrill of the hunt, even the pleasures of opium debauchery pall. When Jasper returns to the Opium Woman's den after a long absence, she cries out in amazement:

"Why, it's you!"

"Are you so surprised to see me?"

"I thought I never should have seen you again, deary. I thought you was dead, and gone to Heaven."

"Why?"

"I didn't suppose you could have kept away, alive, so long, from the poor old soul with the real receipt for mixing it" (Chapter 23).

Jasper has stayed away because the reality of murder is more exhilarating by far than anything she has to offer. Between the slaying of his first victim and the discovery of a new one, he has had little need for opium. But now his hounding of Neville has begun to drag. In the six months or more since Drood's death, he has found no way to fasten the crime on his scapegoat. So back he comes to the opium den, for relief and for a brief respite in his labors.

Backtracking to the first occasion in the novel when uncle and nephew appear together (in Chapter 2), we find a passage that unmistakably reveals the murderer's relish for his grisly enterprise. "Mr. Jasper stands still, and looks on intently at the young fellow, divesting himself of his outward coat, hat, gloves, and so forth. Once for all, a look of intentness and intensity—a look of hungry, exacting, watchful, and yet devoted affection—is always, now and ever afterwards, on the Jasper face whenever the Jasper face is addressed in this direction. And whenever it is so addressed, it is never, on this occasion or on any other, dividedly addressed; it is always concentrated."

There is something frighteningly familiar about this intense look of Jasper's. Where else does one see exactly that expression—hungry, exacting, watchful, and yet (paradoxically) affectionate? It is the look on a cat's face when he plays with a mouse. Never is the cat more intent; never is his expression more concentrated; and never does he display a more devoted affection for one of his fellow creatures; than when he releases the mouse from his cruel claws and watches fascinated as it tries to creep away to safety. Affection? Of course. The cat loves the mouse. Predators evolved to hunt and kill; without our prey we could do neither; and so we love them. In exactly the way John Jasper loves his nephew.

The analogy between mouser and murderer is further reinforced when Jasper, cat-like, plays with his victim, allowing him momentarily an opportunity to escape by warning him of his danger:

" 'You know now, don't you, that even a poor monotonous chorister and grinder of music—in his niche—may be troubled with some stray sort of ambition, aspiration, restlessness, dissatisfaction, what shall we call it?'

" 'Yes, dear Jack.' . . .

" 'Take it as a warning, then.' "

Edwin completely misunderstands the application of these last words, but as the boy replies to his uncle's unexpected admonition, "Mr. Jasper's steadiness of face and figure becomes so marvellous that his breathing seems to have stopped." Like a cat crouching breathless before he springs, the choirmaster watches Edwin for any sign of awareness that the threat is real. When he perceives that his warning has fallen on deaf ears, he becomes "a breathing man again without the smallest stage of transition between the two extreme states."

While Edwin talks at length about his future prospects, "Mr. Jasper, with his hand to his chin, and with an expression of musing benevolence on his face, has attentively watched every animated look and gesture attending the delivery of these words. He remains in that attitude after they are spoken, as if in a kind of fascination attendant on his strong interest in the youthful spirit that he loves so well. Then he says with a quiet smile [while inwardly licking his chops]:

" 'You won't be warned, then?'

" 'No, Jack.'

" 'You can't be warned, then?'

" 'No, Jack, not by you.' "

Why does Jasper warn his nephew at all? Because putting him on his guard adds zest to the blood sport. Bored to distraction by his humdrum existence in Cloisterham, the choirmaster thoroughly enjoys the game of life and death in which he's engaged. In fact he admits as much to the Princess Puffer, to whom he says of his crime, "I did it over and over again. I have done it hundreds of thousands of times. . . . It *was* pleasant to do!" A terrible man indeed!

To commit the perfect crime—to kill someone and get away unsuspected—that's the one great object in Jasper's life. And the murder of Edwin Drood—flawed though it is by Grewgious's disclosure—so delights him that he tries again with a second victim. By pinning the blame for Edwin's death on his rival Landless, Jasper hopes to induce the State to hang Neville for his own crime. What could be more perfect than that?

Chapter XVII

The Wicked Man

A few words about the interrelationships between the theme and plot of *Edwin Drood,* and some brief closing comments, should be sufficient to wrap up my study of Charles Dickens's last novel. In writing *The Mystery of Edwin Drood* it was the author's purpose to present the psychological portrait of a murderer—of John Jasper, the man who killed the nephew he once had loved. In such earlier stories as *Martin Chuzzlewit* and *Our Mutual Friend* Dickens had probed the psyches of murderers, but in neither was the sole or major emphasis of the work on the criminal's mind and motives. Yet clearly the psychology of murder fascinated Dickens, and he saw in the mystery-story form the perfect vehicle to combine an exciting, melodramatic tale with a thorough analysis of the criminal mentality.

That John Jasper is the central character in *Edwin Drood* can hardly be denied. From the opening scene in the opium den, his sinister shadow sets its black mark not just on the sundial but on everyone with whom he comes in contact, and we feel with Rosa "as if he could pass in through the wall when he is spoken of." Just as the story begins with Jasper, so, as Forster has told us, it was to end with Jasper, reluctantly recounting in his condemned cell the wild passions and murderous deeds that brought him there. Mrs. Kate

The Execution of John Thurtell

Dickens Perugini endorsed Forster's account, and added that it was not "upon the Mystery alone that [my father] relied for the interest and originality of his idea. The originality was to be shown, as he tells us, in what we may call the psychological description the murderer gives us of his temptations, temperament, and character. . . . I do not mean to imply that the mystery itself had no strong hold on my father's imagination; but . . . he was quite as deeply fascinated and absorbed in the study of the criminal Jasper, as in the dark and sinister crime that has given the book its title."[1]

The premise underlying Dickens's treatment of John Jasper was his frequently expressed conviction that a murderer has a diseased mind—that his mentality is different in kind from that of ordinary men. In "Hunted Down" he declares emphatically, "It is a sort of fashion to express surprise that any notorious criminal, having such crime upon his conscience, can so brave it out. Do you think that if he had it on his conscience at all, or had a conscience to have it upon, he would ever have committed the crime?" Even more to the point is his statement in *Edwin Drood* itself: "What could she [Rosa] know of the criminal intellect, which its own professed students perpetually misread, because they persist in trying to reconcile it with the average intellect of average men, instead of identifying it as a horrible wonder apart."

Perceiving *The Mystery of Edwin Drood* as the character analysis of a murderer helps direct us toward the novel's theme, which has its source in the distinctive *symptom* of criminal irrationality. Because the murderer has an unbalanced mind, *he will invariably overreach himself;* he will not be able to stop after his first crime, but will go on and on until inevitably he drives himself to his own destruction. This theme was to be worked out in the story by the actions of John Jasper after the murder of his nephew. If the choirmaster had not demanded a second sacrifice to his passions, he would never have been caught; but in pursuing Neville he brings into play forces that were in the end to crush him.

The *means* of his undoing is of course the ring with its "rose of diamonds and rubies delicately set in gold," which Drood had in his possession when he was murdered. As Montagu Saunders suggests, Jasper returns to Mrs. Sapsea's tomb to recover this ring because he intends to use it as the "one wanting link" in his chain of evidence against Neville.[2] Believing that the body would never be found, and feeling certain that there was no evidence against him even if it were found, Jasper has no need for the ring except as an instrument for entrapping his scapegoat; and retrieving it and planting it on Landless appears to involve no risk at all to Jasper himself. To the reader it would have seemed—at the critical moment when Bazzard tells Jasper about the ring and the latter rushes off to fetch it—that the murderer's vicious scheme was about to succeed. But then, completely reversing the fortunes of Neville and Jasper, was to come the dramatic confrontation in the tomb.

Yet the final victory of justice is made possible only by the intervention of Helena Landless. It was clearly Helena, in her "Defiance of all suspicion, and unbounded faith in her brother" (*ED,* Chapter 15), who first prompted Hiram Grewgious to look to John Jasper for the explanation of Edwin's sudden disappearance, and who thereby set in motion the long train of pursuit that led ultimately to Jasper's apprehension. And it was to be Helena who would triumphantly conclude that pursuit by facing Jasper in his cell and forcing him to confess—a dangerous mission which she undertook not to avenge Edwin Drood, whom she rather despised (she once called his spirit "trivial"), but to exonerate her twin brother. Helena's impersonation is essential, because it is her striking physical resemblance to Neville that convinces Jasper he is seeing a ghost, and so brings about his defeat. If the murderer had not attempted to incriminate an innocent man for his crime, his most effective adversary would have had no motive for entering the fray against him.

In earlier chapters I've touched upon Dickens's fascination for John Thurtell, whose murder of William Weare in 1823 (when Dickens was an impressionable boy of eleven) intrigued the novelist for the rest of his days. Like John Jasper, Thurtell was a young man of good family and considerable natural gifts who went from bad to worse to the murder of a friend who trusted him.[3] After a lifetime of pondering over Thurtell and other homicides, Dickens intended to put everything he had to say about murderers into his final novel, *The Mystery of Edwin Drood.* His psychological study of the murderer John Jasper would have enabled the author to illustrate his strongly held belief that the criminal mentality, being "a horrible wonder apart," causes the wrongdoer to go too far, and so leads him to his ruin. Dickens masterfully worked out this theme in the novel by making Jasper the chief agent in his own downfall, thus demonstrating the novelist's pet theory that even "the most clever criminals were constantly detected through some small defect in their calculations."

Yet it is possible that there is a theme behind this obvious theme, an underlying message that Dickens intended to bring to the fore in his closing chapters. This deeper motif, stated simply, is that God can forgive what man cannot. It is hinted at as early as the first chapter, when Dickens "touches the key-note" with the opening phrase from this verse of the prophet Ezekiel: "When the wicked man turneth away from his wickedness that he hath committed, and doeth that which is lawful and right, he shall save his soul alive."[4] And it is subtly suggested again in a sentence from the final chapter of the *Drood* fragment: "Changes of glorious light from moving boughs, songs of birds, scents from gardens, woods, and fields—or rather, from the one great garden of the whole cultivated island in its yielding time—penetrate into the Cathedral, subdue its earthy odour, and preach the Resurrection and the Life." This is an odd comment to make just as Drood's avengers begin to close in on the killer—for moments later the Opium Woman gives Dick Datchery his first glimpse behind Jasper's cloak of respectability. Thus we are reminded of the Resurrection and the Life precisely when Jasper's defeat and death are first foreshadowed.

Dickens's choice of Christmas Eve for the occurrence of pivotal events in his story may also have special significance. Durdles hears his ghost sounds on a Christmas Eve, Drood disappears on the next Christmas Eve, and Jasper (perhaps) was to be apprehended on the following Christmas Eve. Of Drood's slaying Richard Baker writes, "And now it is Christmas Eve in Cloisterham—the eve of that Holy Birthday of which Dickens had so often extolled the sacred and festive spirit in his Christmas books and stories. By some strange revulsion of feeling he now casts aside his 'Carol' philosophy to choose December 25th as the day for Edwin Drood's murder."[5] But was it revulsion or thematic purpose that led Dickens to select the day of the Savior's birth for key incidents in the novel?

So it may be that the choirmaster, shocked into catharsis by his experience with Helena Landless, was at last to repent of his crimes and seek God's forgiveness. True, the typical Dickensian murderer, like Jonas Chuzzlewit or Bradley Headstone, is concerned not with contrition but only with how he can save his skin; a remorseful villain would have been a radical departure for the author—another "new idea," if you will, and exceedingly difficult for Dickens to work successfully. While there is no way now to determine with certainty whether Jasper was to turn away from his wickedness and save his soul alive, the confrontation scene with Helena, providing as it does a reason for his last-minute conversion, at least creates that possibility.

Whether *long-lost relationships* were to play an important part in the plot is another of *The Mystery*'s more intractable puzzles. Certainly the book contains abundant potential for such secret ties. Rosa Bud is an orphan with no living relative "that she knew of in the world." Drood's father and mother died some years before the story begins, and we are told nothing about Jasper's parents. Could Rosa, or Edwin and Jasper, be related to someone else whom we've met in the narrative? Neville and Helena were reared by a cruel stepfather. Is their natural father a character in the novel? Once we start playing with such conjectures, the possibilities are almost limitless. Are the twins somehow related—irony of ironies—to John Jasper? Whose child is Deputy? Where does Dick Datchery fit in? No doubt any one of the book's characters could bear some undisclosed relationship to any other, but there is simply not enough evidence in the half-finished novel to establish any of the dubious combinations proposed by other commentators. Before we fall back on such a treacherous resource to resolve our difficulties, we ought to probe the text more deeply to try to find alternative answers.

Which brings me to the Princess Puffer. Numerous writers have suggested that she is related in some way to John Jasper because she hates the choirmaster and takes the trouble to trace him to his lair in Cloisterham. They believe her behavior only makes sense if some hidden relationship exists between herself and the villain; but in fact both her hatred and her pursuit can be explained by a careful reading of the novel as we have it, without resorting to romantic fantasies about her past life.

Why does she hate Jasper? Consider first this exchange from Chapter 23 between the Princess and the clerk at Jasper's London hotel. She asks:

"Is the gentleman from Cloisterham indoors?"

"Just gone out."

"Unlucky. When does the gentleman return to Cloisterham?"

"At six this evening."

"Bless ye and thank ye. May the Lord prosper a business where a civil question, even from a poor soul, is so civilly answered!"

In other words, "Treat me decently and I'll respond in kind." Contrast this to a conversation with Jasper in the same chapter. Again she leads with a question:

"Who was they as died, deary?"

"A relative."

"Died of what, lovey?"

"Probably, Death."

"We are short to-night!" cries the woman, with a propitiatory laugh. "Short and snappish we are!"

This passage sets the tone for their ensuing dialogue, during which Jasper never misses a chance to display his contempt for her.

Later that night, when he has fallen into an incoherent stupor, she croaks under her breath, "I heard ye say once, when I was lying where you're lying, *and you were making your speculations upon me,* 'Unintelligible!' I heard you say so, of two more than me. But don't ye be too sure always; don't ye be too sure, beauty!" (Emphasis added.)

She refers, of course, to Jasper's earlier visit to her den, recounted in the first chapter. On that occasion he indulged in these "speculations" upon his hostess after she had passed out (or so he thought): "What visions can *she* have? . . . Visions of many butchers' shops, and public-houses, and much credit? Of an increase of hideous customers, and this horrible bedstead set upright again, and this horrible court swept clean? What can she rise to, under any quantity of opium, higher than that!—Eh?"

Now suppose the woman heard all this, as she certainly implies in *her* speculations over *his* unconscious form. Is it any wonder she hates Jasper? Wouldn't you hate someone who told you your aspirations could rise no higher than visions of butchers' shops?

And Deputy hates Jasper for pretty much the same reason. At their first meeting, in Chapter 5, the choirmaster calls the boy a "Baby-Devil"; refers to him in his hearing as "this thing" and "This creature"; and snarls at him, "don't throw while I stand so near him, or I'll kill you!" The wicked man has a special knack for alienating those beneath him on the social ladder, a propensity he refrains from only in the case of Durdles—but of course he needs the stonemason's assistance to further his schemes.

Given that the Puffer hates Jasper, why does she follow him to Cloisterham? Blackmail, asserts Richard Baker,[6] and I agree. From his dress and his speech, it is obvious to her that Jasper, unlike her other customers, is a member of respectable society—a gentleman, and by her standards a man of means. From what she has heard him say in his drugged ramblings, she knows he has threatened, and later done away with, someone named Ned. This makes him vulnerable to blackmail, and the Opium Woman loves money even more than she hates Jasper. Therefore she tracks him down to learn who he is and exactly what he has done, for she sees blackmail as the perfect means of gratifying both her lust for lucre and her thirst for revenge.

Before closing, I have a few words to say about the fragmentary composition entitled (by John Forster) "How Mr. Sapsea ceased to be a Member of the Eight Club." It has always been my belief that this unfinished story was written sometime before Dickens began working on *Edwin Drood,* and that it contributes nothing to a solution of the mystery—except for revealing where the author found the names and occupations of the auctioneer Mr. Sapsea and the schoolmistress Miss Twinkleton. Even the notion that Poker served as a study for Dick Datchery is debatable, for that young flatterer (who strikes me as some sort of confidence man) can more readily be seen as a precursor of the 26-year-old lawbreaker Jasper than of the white-haired lawman Datchery. In a recent article Charles Forsyte has confirmed my opinion about the date of the fragment's composition. By a painstaking examination of the "Sapsea" manuscript and other original documents, Mr. Forsyte has established that Dickens wrote it two or three years before he started *Edwin Drood,*[7] a conclusion that demonstrates its uselessness as a source of enlightenment about the novel's plot.

Unlike most *Drood* commentators, to make my case I have relied less on evidence in *The Mystery* itself, and more on material from Dickens's other works and from other contemporary writings. There is a reason for this somewhat unorthodox approach. The author concealed his intentions so skillfully in *Edwin Drood* that almost any conclusion one chooses, however farfetched, can be supported by citations from the novel. While a great deal of progress has been made, over the past hundred-and-some years, in penetrating the riddle of Edwin Drood's disappearance, an impasse had been reached on several issues, most notably on that of Dick Datchery's identity. By considering more diversified sources than most, from the cornucopia of Victorian mystery fiction to the history of the Metropolitan Police, I hoped to break through this barrier and provide some new leads to the solution of *The Mystery of Edwin Drood.* My readers must now judge for themselves whether this effort has succeeded.

Exhibits

Exhibit A

THE PLOT OF "EDWIN DROOD"
by
J. Cuming Walters
(Abridged)

Edwin Drood and Rosa Bud were betrothed by their dead parents. They grew up liking each other, but were not in love.

John Jasper, Drood's uncle, only a few years his elder, is madly in love with Rosa. She knows it, and fears him. Jasper is a musician, and as Lay Precentor at Cloisterham Cathedral is much respected; but secretly he is addicted to the opium vice, and haunts a den in London.

Jasper affects the most extravagant regard for Edwin Drood, but none the less is jealous of him, *and appears to be plotting against him.*

A pompous auctioneer named Sapsea has lately buried his wife. Jasper spends an evening with him, and is introduced to an eccentric drunken mason, "Stony" Durdles, who has the keys of the crypt and the tombs. Jasper handles the keys, clinks them together, and detects the peculiar sound given out by the one that unlocks the Sapsea vault. Thus he would, if in the dark, know the key by its weight and sound.

But Durdles gives Jasper the unexpected and startling information that he can by tapping with his hammer tell whether any vault contains one body or two, and whether the corpse has turned to dust or not. Jasper consequently inquires into the action of quicklime, which, he is told, will consume everything—except metal.

Whenever Durdles is out "arter ten" he is pelted home by a boy called "Deputy"—a gamin connected with a cheap lodging house. Jasper is greatly enraged on encountering this watchful boy, and they regard each other with the greatest antipathy.

New characters are now introduced—Neville and Helena Landless, twins, who have had a wild and unhappy youth in Ceylon with a harsh stepfather, and are brought by an aggressive self-styled philanthropist, Mr. Honeythunder, to Mr. Crisparkle, Minor Canon, to be disciplined and educated. Neville, resenting Drood's cool treatment of Rosa (with whom he falls in love at first sight), quarrels with him. Jasper adroitly foments the ill-feeling, and then reports to the Canon that Neville is dangerous, and that Edwin's life is in jeopardy.

In the meantime Edwin and Rosa, after consultation with Mr. Grewgious, Rosa's "angular," old-fashioned, good-hearted family solicitor and guardian, decide to break off their engagement. Jasper is not told because Edwin thinks the news would distress him.

Grewgious had given to Edwin a ring—"a rose of diamonds and rubies delicately set in gold"—to place on Rosa's finger if the marriage were fixed. This Edwin now retains, and it is the one piece of jewellery in his possession of which Jasper knows nothing.

* * * * *

Jasper next visits the Crypt with Durdles, who tells him of a strange dream he had the previous Christmas Eve, when he heard "the ghost of a cry." Jasper drugs Durdles, *watches him fall asleep, and then leaves him for a considerable time.* Dickens calls this "the unaccountable expedition."

An arrangement is made for Neville and Edwin to meet at Christmas Eve at Jasper's house and end their feud.

On that day Edwin meets in Cloisterham an old opium woman, who says she is searching for someone, and tells him that "Ned," which Jasper alone calls him, is "a threatened name."

Neville prepares to start on a lonely walking tour on the morrow.

At night, a night of terrific storm, the meeting takes place; in the morning Drood has disappeared.

Jasper at once accuses Neville, who had been with Edwin to the riverside at midnight, of murder. The case breaks down for want of evidence, but a dark suspicion remains. Neville goes to London, and takes a room near Mr. Grewgious's chambers. His sister remains for a time in Cloisterham, and lives down malignity.

Canon Crisparkle finds Drood's watch and chain and scarf pin in the river. This confirms the suspicion of foul play. Jasper resolves to devote himself to finding and destroying the murderer.

Grewgious tells Jasper of the broken engagement. The news has an extraordinary effect on him, and he swoons.

* * * * *

When some months have passed a mysterious stranger arrives in Cloisterham. He has *a large head, white hair,* and black eyebrows. His name is Dick Datchery, "an idle buffer living on his means." He takes lodgings at Tope's, next to Jasper's, and at once makes the latter's acquaintance.

Jasper now boldly avows his love to Rosa. She flies to Grewgious. He for some time has been observing Jasper's stealthy visits to London.

An arrangement is made whereby Rosa and Helena can meet unobserved in the rooms of a young sailor, Mr. Tartar.

The story pauses whilst an amusing description is given of Rosa's experience with Mrs. Billickin in lodgings, and of Mr. Grewgious's curious relationship with his clerk, Bazzard, the unsuccessful writer of a tragedy.

We next trace Jasper back to the opium den, babbling to the eagerly listening old woman of a strange journey he undertook with a companion. She tries to learn more from him, but fails, and follows him to Cloisterham. There she meets Datchery and informs him of her previous meeting with Edwin Drood. She inquires after Jasper, goes to the Cathedral, hears him sing, and menaces him with her fist. Datchery observes this, and as he is keeping an account of all he learns by the old-fashioned tavern method of chalk marks, he goes home and "adds one thick line to the score."

And here the story abruptly ends.

Exhibit B

Excerpts from THE DETECTIVE POLICE by Charles Dickens

We are not by any means devout believers in the old Bow Street Police. To say the truth, we think there was a vast amount of humbug about those worthies. Apart from many of them being men of very indifferent character, and far too much in the habit of consorting with thieves and the like, they never lost a public occasion of jobbing and trading in mystery and making the most of themselves. Continually puffed besides by incompetent magistrates anxious to conceal their own deficiencies, and hand-in-glove with the penny-a-liners of that time, they became a sort of superstition. Although as a Preventive Police they were utterly ineffective, and as a Detective Police were very loose and uncertain in their operations, they remain with some people a superstition to the present day.

On the other hand, the Detective Force organised since the establishment of the existing Police, is so well chosen and trained, proceeds so systematically and quietly, does its business in such a workmanlike manner, and is always so calmly and steadily engaged in the service of the public, that the public really do not know enough of it, to know a tithe of its usefulness. Impressed with this conviction, and interested in the men themselves, we represented to the authorities at Scotland Yard, that we should be glad, if there were no official objection, to have some talk with the Detectives. A most obliging and ready permission being given, a certain evening was appointed with a certain Inspector for a social conference between ourselves and the Detectives, at The Household Words Office in Wellington Street, Strand, London. In consequence of which appointment the party "came off," which we are about to describe. And we beg to repeat that, avoiding such topics as it might for obvious reasons be injurious to the public, or disagreeable to respectable individuals, to touch upon in print, our description is as exact as we can make it.

The reader will have the goodness to imagine the Sanctum Sanctorum of Household Words. Anything that best suits the reader's fancy, will best represent that magnificent chamber. We merely stipulate for a round table in the middle, with some glasses and cigars arranged upon it; and the editorial sofa elegantly hemmed in between that stately piece of furniture and the wall.

Just at dusk, Inspectors Wield and Stalker are announced; but we do not undertake to warrant the orthography of any of the names here mentioned. Inspector Wield presents Inspector Stalker. Inspector Wield is a middle-aged man of a portly presence, with a large, moist, knowing eye, a husky voice, and a habit of emphasising his conversation by the aid of a corpulent fore-finger, which is constantly in juxta-position with his eyes or nose. Inspector Stalker is a shrewd, hard-headed Scotchman—in appearance not at all unlike a very acute, thoroughly-trained schoolmaster, from the Normal Establishment at Glasgow. Inspector Wield one might have known, perhaps, for what he is—Inspector Stalker, never.

The ceremonies of reception over, Inspectors Wield and Stalker observe that they have brought some sergeants with them. The sergeants are presented—five in number, Sergeant Dornton, Sergeant Witchem, Sergeant Mith, Sergeant Fendall, and Sergeant Straw. We have the whole Detective Force from Scotland Yard, with one exception. They sit down in a semi-circle (the two Inspectors at the two ends) at a little distance from the round table, facing the editorial sofa. Every man of them, in a glance, immediately takes an inventory of the furniture and an accurate sketch of the editorial presence. The Editor feels that any gentleman in company could take him up, if need should be, without the smallest hesitation, twenty years hence.

The whole party are in plain clothes. Sergeant Dornton about fifty years of age, with a ruddy face and a high sunburnt forehead, has the air of one who has been a Sergeant in the army—he might have sat to Wilkie for the Soldier in the Reading of the Will. He is famous for steadily pursuing the inductive process, and, from small beginnings, working on from clue to clue until he bags his man. Sergeant Witchem, shorter and thicker-set, and marked with the small-pox, has something of a reserved and thoughtful air, as if he were engaged in deep arithmetical calculations. He is renowned for his acquaintance with the swell mob. Sergeant Mith, a smooth-faced man with a fresh bright complexion, and a strange air of simplicity, is a dab at housebreakers. Sergeant Fendall, a light-haired, well-spoken, polite person, is a prodigious hand at pursuing private inquiries of a delicate nature. Straw, a little wiry Sergeant of meek demeanour and strong sense, would knock at a door and ask a series of questions in any mild character you choose to prescribe to him, from a charity-boy upwards, and seem as innocent as an infant. They are, one and all, respectable-looking men; of perfectly good deportment and unusual intelligence; with nothing lounging or slinking in their manners; with an air of keen observation and quick perception when addressed; and generally presenting in their faces, traces more or less marked of habitually leading lives of strong mental excitement. They have all good eyes; and they all can, and they all do, look full at whomsoever they speak to.

We light the cigars, and hand round the glasses (which are very temperately used indeed), and the conversation begins by a modest amateur reference on the Editorial part to the swell mob. Inspector Wield immediately removes his cigar from his lips, waves his right hand, and says, "Regarding the swell mob, sir, I can't do better than call upon Sergeant Witchem. Because the reason why? I'll tell you. Sergeant Witchem is better acquainted with the swell mob than any officer in London."

Our heart leaping up when we beheld this rainbow in the sky, we turn to Sergeant Witchem, who very concisely, and in well-chosen language, goes into the subject forthwith. Meantime, the whole of his brother officers are closely interested in attending to what he says, and observing its effect. Presently they begin to strike in, one or two together, when an opportunity offers, and the conversation becomes general. But these brother officers only come in to the assistance of each other—not to the contradiction—and a more amicable brotherhood there could not be. From the swell mob, we diverge to the kindred topics of cracksmen, fences, public-house dancers, area-sneaks, designing young people who go out "gonophing," and other "schools." It is observable throughout these revelations, that Inspector Stalker, the Scotchman, is always exact and statistical, and that when any question of figures arises, everybody as by one consent pauses, and looks to him.

From these topics, we glide into a review of the most celebrated and horrible of the great crimes that have been committed within the last fifteen or twenty years. The men engaged in the discovery of almost all of them, and in the pursuit or apprehension of the murderers, are here, down to the very last instance. One of our guests gave chase to and boarded the emigrant ship, in which the murderess last hanged in London was supposed to have embarked. We learn from him that his errand was not announced to the passengers, who may have no idea of it to this hour. That he went below, with the captain, lamp in hand—it being dark, and the whole steerage abed and sea-sick—and engaged the Mrs. Manning who *was* on board, in a conversation about her luggage, until she was, with no small pains, induced to raise her head, and turn her face towards the light. Satisfied that she was not the object of his search, he quietly re-embarked in the Government steamer alongside, and steamed home again with the intelligence.

* * * * *

It being now late, and the party very modest in their fear of being too diffuse, there were some tokens of separation; when Sergeant Dornton, the soldierly-looking man, said, looking round him with a smile:

"Before we break up, sir, perhaps you might have some amusement in hearing of the Adventures of a Carpet Bag. They are very short; and, I think, curious."

We welcomed the Carpet Bag cordially, and Sergeant Dornton proceeded.

"In 1847, I was despatched to Chatham, in search of one Mesheck, a Jew. He had been carrying on, pretty heavily, in the bill-stealing way, getting acceptances from young men of good connexions (in the army chiefly), on pretence of discount, and bolting with the same.

"Mesheck was off, before I got to Chatham. All I could learn about him was, that he had gone, probably to London, and had with him—a Carpet Bag.

"I came back to town, by the last train from Blackwall, and made inquiries concerning a Jew passenger with—a Carpet Bag.

"The office was shut up, it being the last train. There were only two or three porters left. Looking after a Jew with a Carpet Bag, on the Blackwall Railway, which was then the high road to a great Military Depot, was worse than looking after a needle in a hayrick. But it happened that one of these porters had carried, for a certain Jew, to a certain public-house, a certain—Carpet Bag.

"I went to the public-house, but the Jew had only left his luggage there for a few hours, and had called for it in a cab, and taken it away. I put such questions there, and to the porter, as I thought prudent, and got at this description of—the Carpet Bag.

"It was a bag which had, on one side of it, worked in worsted, a green parrot on a stand. A green parrot on a stand was the means by which to identify that—Carpet Bag.

"I traced Mesheck, by means of this green parrot on a stand, to Cheltenham, to Birmingham, to Liverpool, to the Atlantic Ocean. At Liverpool he was too many for me. He had gone to the United States, and I gave up all thoughts of Mesheck, and likewise of his—Carpet Bag.

"Many months afterwards—near a year afterwards—there was a bank in Ireland robbed of seven thousand pounds, by a person of the name of Doctor Dundey, who escaped to America; from which country some of the stolen notes came home. He was supposed to have bought a farm in New Jersey. Under proper management, that estate could be seized and sold, for the benefit of the parties he had defrauded. I was sent off to America for this purpose.

"I landed at Boston. I went on to New York. I found that he had lately changed New York paper-money for New Jersey paper-money, and had banked cash in New Brunswick. To take this Doctor Dundey, it was necessary to entrap him into the State of New York, which required a deal of artifice and trouble. At one time, he couldn't be drawn into an appointment. At another time, he appointed to come to meet me, and a New York officer, on a pretext I made; and then his children had the measles. At last he came, per steamboat, and I took him, and lodged him in a New York prison called the Tombs; which I dare say you know, sir?"

Editorial acknowledgment to that effect.

"I went to the Tombs, on the morning after his capture, to attend the examination before the magistrate. I was passing through the magistrate's private room, when, happening to look round me to take notice of the place, as we generally have a habit of doing, I clapped my eyes, in one corner, on a—Carpet Bag.

"What did I see upon that Carpet Bag, if you'll believe me, but a green parrot on a stand, as large as life!

" 'That Carpet Bag, with the representation of a green parrot on a stand,' said I, 'belongs to an English Jew, name Aaron Mesheck, and to no other man, alive or dead!'

"I give you my word the New York Police Officers were doubled up with surprise.

" 'How did you ever come to know that?' said they.

" 'I think I ought to know that green parrot by this time,' said I; 'for I have had as pretty a dance after that bird, at home, as ever I had, in all my life!' "

"And was it Mesheck's?" we submissively inquired.

"Was it, sir? Of course it was! He was in custody for another offence, in that very identical Tombs, at that very identical time. And, more than that! Some memoranda, relating to the fraud for which I had vainly endeavoured to take him, were found to be, at that moment, lying in that very same individual—Carpet Bag!"

Thus, at midnight, closed the proceedings of our curious and interesting party. But one other circumstance finally wound up the evening, after our Detective guests had left us. One of the sharpest among them, and the officer best acquainted with the Swell Mob, had his pocket picked, going home!

Exhibit C

THE SOFA
by
Charles Dickens

"What young men will do, sometimes, to ruin themselves and break their friends' hearts," said Sergeant Dornton, "it's surprising! I had a case at Saint Blank's Hospital which was of this sort. A bad case, indeed, with a bad end!

"The Secretary, and the House-Surgeon, and the Treasurer, of Saint Blank's Hospital, came to Scotland Yard to give information of numerous robberies having been committed on the students. The students could leave nothing in the pockets of their great-coats, while the great-coats were hanging at the hospital, but it was almost certain to be stolen. Property of various descriptions was constantly being lost; and the gentlemen were naturally uneasy about it, and anxious, for the credit of the institution, that the thief or thieves should be discovered. The case was entrusted to me, and I went to the hospital.

" 'Now, gentlemen,' said I, after we had talked it over, 'I understand this property is usually lost from one room.'

"Yes, they said. It was.

" 'I should wish, if you please,' said I, 'to see the room.'

"It was a good-sized bare room down-stairs, with a few tables and forms in it, and a row of pegs, all round, for hats and coats.

" 'Next, gentlemen,' said I, 'do you suspect anybody?'

"Yes, they said. They did suspect somebody. They were sorry to say, they suspected one of the porters.

" 'I should like,' said I, 'to have that man pointed out to me, and to have a little time to look after him.'

"He was pointed out, and I looked after him, and then I went back to the hospital, and said, 'Now, gentlemen, it's not the porter. He's, unfortunately for himself, a little too fond of drink, but he's nothing worse. My suspicion is, that these robberies are committed by one of the students; and if you'll put me a sofa into that room where the pegs are—as there's no closet—I think I shall be able to detect the thief. I wish the sofa, if you please, to be covered with chintz, or something of that sort, so that I may lie on my chest, underneath it, without being seen.'

"The sofa was provided, and next day at eleven o'clock, before any of the students came, I went there, with those gentlemen, to get underneath it. It turned out to be one of those old-fashioned sofas with a great cross-beam at the bottom, that would have broken my back in no time if I could ever have got below it. We had quite a job to break all this away in the time; however, I fell to work, and they fell to work, and we broke it out, and made a clear place for me. I got under the sofa, lay down on my chest, took out my knife, and made a convenient hole in the chintz to look through. It was then settled between me and the gentlemen that when the students were all up in the wards, one of the gentlemen should come in, and hang up a great-coat on one of the pegs. And that that great-coat should have, in one of the pockets, a pocket-book containing marked money.

"After I had been there some time, the students began to drop into the room, by ones, and twos, and threes, and to talk about all sorts of things, little thinking there was anybody under the sofa—and then to go up-stairs. At last there came in one who remained until he was alone in the room by himself. A tallish, good-looking young man of one or two and twenty, with a light whisker. He went to a particular hat-peg, took off a good hat that was hanging there, tried it on, hung his own hat in its place, and hung that hat on another peg, nearly opposite to me. I then felt quite certain that he was the thief, and would come back by-and-by.

"When they were all up-stairs, the gentleman came in with the great-coat. I showed him where to hang it, so that I might have a good view of it; and he went away; and I lay under the sofa on my chest, for a couple of hours or so, waiting.

"At last, the same young man came down. He walked across the room, whistling—stopped and listened—took another walk and whistled—stopped again and listened—then began to go regularly round the pegs, feeling in the pockets of all the coats. When he came to THE great-coat, and felt the pocket-book, he was so eager and so hurried that he broke the strap in tearing it open. As he began to put the money in his pocket, I crawled out from under the sofa, and his eyes met mine.

"My face, as you may perceive, is brown now, but it was pale at that time, my health not being good; and looked as long as a horse's. Besides which, there was a great draught of air from the door, underneath the sofa, and I had tied a handkerchief round my head; so what I looked like, altogether, I don't know. He turned blue—literally blue—when he saw me crawling out, and I couldn't feel surprised at it.

" 'I am an officer of the Detective Police,' said I, 'and have been lying here, since you first came in this morning. I regret, for the sake of yourself and your friends, that you should have done what you have; but this case is complete. You have the pocket-book in your hand and the money upon you; and I must take you into custody!'

"It was impossible to make out any case in his behalf, and on his trial he pleaded guilty. How or when he got the means I don't know; but while he was awaiting his sentence, he poisoned himself in Newgate."

We inquired of this officer, on the conclusion of the foregoing anecdote, whether the time appeared long, or short, when he lay in that constrained position under the sofa?

"Why, you see, sir," he replied, "if he hadn't come in, the first time, and I had not been quite sure he was the thief, and would return, the time would have seemed long. But, as it was, I being dead certain of my man, the time seemed pretty short."

Exhibit D

THE DATE OF THE STORY
by
Percy Carden

The murder took place precisely at midnight, 24–25 December, 1842. The reader is no doubt astonished at this confident assertion. So was the author to discover the evidence on which he bases it.

Speaking approximately, the book itself proves the disappearance to have been on a Christmas Eve which was a Saturday. If any precise year was intended, therefore, it must have been one in which Christmas Day fell upon a Sunday. We can narrow the choice of year still further. In those days there was no railway to Cloisterham, and Mr. Sapsea said there never would be. Some remote fragment of main line to somewhere else, there was. Now Christmas fell upon a Sunday in 1836, in 1842 and in 1853. In 1836 no remote fragment of line to anywhere else approached near Rochester. By 1853 the line to Strood was built. The line to Strood cannot have been the "fragment" referred to. It was not remote. It was not a fragment of main line to anywhere else. It could not have so unsettled Rochester traffic that the traffic deserting the high road, came sneaking in from an unprecedented part of the country by a back stable way. If any precise year was intended therefore, it can only have been 1842. But was it?

In the year of the book (if it had a year), no neighbouring architecture of lofty proportions had arisen to overshadow Staple Inn. The Westering sun bestowed bright glances on it and the South-west wind blew into it unimpeded. By 1853, this was no longer so. The lofty building which is now the Patent Office standing in what was once the garden of the Inn was planned in 1843, and built soon after. Later the Birkbeck Buildings shut out the Western sun.

Six months or so after the murder, Mr. Crisparkle and Neville dined together in London and then parted at the yet unfinished and undeveloped railway station; Mr. Crisparkle to get home to Rochester. The British Almanac for the previous year, 1842, contains this entry: "The great station at London Bridge, for the joint use of the Brighton, South Eastern and Croydon companies, and the works connected with it, are in rapid progress, but any description of them must be deferred until their completion."

Finally. By 1842, a fragment of the Main Line to Maidstone had been completed and was in use as far as a station then called "Maidstone Road," which will be seen from the map to be the point on that line nearest to Rochester. "I lost ye last, where that omnibus you got into nigh your journey's end plied betwixt the station and the place," the opium woman apostrophises Jasper. Maidstone Road was "the station," and Rochester "the place." The omnibus containing Jasper came sneaking in to Rochester from this unprecedented part of the country (the new railway station) by a back stable way which was then Crow or Crau Lane, but is now the Maidstone Road.

The year 1842, then, is a probable year; it is the only possible year; and it is a year which accords in a quite remarkable fashion with a number of hints contained in the book. In fact the assertion is justified that 1842 was the year intended by Dickens.

Exhibit E

THE "MYSTERY" SOLVED
by
Augustin Daly

At intervals during the last ten months it may have been observed that a dramatization of "*The Mystery of Edwin Drood,*" was underlined by Mr. DALY. Finally as the last season drew near its close, the announcement was withdrawn, and not since repeated. The reason for this will probably always be to the public a sort of sub-mystery to the Mystery itself. Mr. DALY certainly had his reasons, and lest some might suppose that his prospectus of the work was simply one of those florid promises which authors and managers too frequently indulge in, with never a serious intention of fulfilling, this brief chapter is written.

Upon assuming the labor of making a play of Mr. DICKENS' unfinished work, Mr. DALY went to work ardently to obtain a clue to the novelist's intention, and thus to produce the most satisfactory and correct ending obtainable for the drama. With this in view, a letter of general enquiry was addressed to Mr. DICKENS' son. Young Mr. DICKENS replied that the "Mystery of Edwin Drood" was "as great a mystery to him as it was to the public at large." This scarcely satisfied Mr. DALY, though it silenced him for a time. He then conceived the idea that as the illustrated title page of the unfinished story embraced a number of scenes which none of the printed chapters of the work explained, the artist who drew those scenes must hold the lost clue. Mr. DICKENS must have explained his views and desires to him, and he must be able to identify the various figures in the various groups; so the next mail took a letter to Mr. S. L. FILDES from Mr. DALY, questioning that gentleman about his drawings upon that same title page. Some time passed before Mr. FILDES' reply came and when it did it furnished only the following information, putting Mr. DALY, however, on the right track:

"Mr. CHARLES COLLINS, the late Mr. DICKENS' son-in-law, is the gentleman who made the design (for the cover), and in referring you to him I have no doubt you will be able to get information to your satisfaction."

As may be naturally supposed, Mr. DALY did not delay long in addressing Mr. COLLINS, (brother of the distinguished novelist Mr. WILKIE COLLINS), and from Mr. COLLINS the following very interesting and satisfactory answer came with welcome speed, completely

CLEARING UP THE "MYSTERY,"

and as the letter has its own unique literary interest and value, Mr. DALY presents it here without abridgement:

BROMPTON, May 4, 1871.

DEAR SIR:

The late Mr. DICKENS communicated to me some general outlines for his scheme of "Edwin Drood," but it was at a very early stage in the development of the idea, and what he said bore mainly upon the earlier portions of the tale.

Edwin Drood was *never to re-appear*, he having been murdered by Jasper. The girl Rosa not having been really attached to Edwin was not to lament his loss very long, and was, I believe, to admit the sailor, Mr. Tartar, to supply his place. It was intended that Jasper himself should urge on the search after Edwin Drood and the pursuit of his murderer, thus endeavoring to direct suspicion from himself, the real murderer. This is indicated in the design on the right side of the cover of the figures hurrying up the spiral staircase, emblematical of a pursuit. They are led on by Jasper, who points unconsciously to his own figure in the drawing at the head of the title. The female figure at the left of the cover reading the placard "Lost" is only intended to illustrate the doubt entertained by Rosa Budd as to the fate of her lover, Drood. The group beneath it indicates the acceptance of another suitor.

As to anything further it must be purely conjectional. It seems likely that Rosa would marry Mr. Tartar, and possible that the same destiny might await Mr. Crisparkle and Helena Landless. Young Landless himself was to die perhaps, and Jasper certainly would, though whether by falling into the hands of justice or by suicide, or through taking an overdose of opium, which seems most likely, it is impossible to say.

I regret not to be able to afford you more information, and also that your letter should have remained so long unanswered.

Very faithfully yours,

CHARLES ALLSTON COLLINS.

Exhibit F

LAST BOOK
by
John Forster

The last book undertaken by Dickens was to be published in illustrated monthly numbers, of the old form, but to close with the twelfth. It closed, unfinished, with the sixth number, which was itself underwritten by two pages.

His first fancy for the tale was expressed in a letter in the middle of July. "What should you think of the idea of a story beginning in this way?—Two people, boy and girl, or very young, going apart from one another, pledged to be married after many years—at the end of the book. The interest to arise out of the tracing of their separate ways, and the impossibility of telling what will be done with that impending fate." This was laid aside; but it left a marked trace on the story as afterwards designed, in the position of Edwin Drood and his betrothed.

I first heard of the later design in a letter dated "Friday the 6th of August 1869," in which after speaking, with the usual unstinted praise he bestowed always on what moved him in others, of a little tale he had received for his journal, he spoke of the change that had occurred to him for the new tale by himself. "I laid aside the fancy I told you of, and have a very curious and new idea for my new story. Not a communicable idea (or the interest of the book would be gone), but a very strong one, though difficult to work." The story, I learnt immediately afterward, was to be that of the murder of a nephew by his uncle; the originality of which was to consist in the review of the murderer's career by himself at the close, when its temptations were to be dwelt upon as if, not he the culprit, but some other man, were the tempted. The last chapters were to be written in the condemned cell, to which his wickedness, all elaborately elicited from him as if told of another, had brought him. Discovery by the murderer of the utter needlessness of the murder for its object was to follow hard upon commission of the deed; but all discovery of the murderer was to be baffled till towards the close, when, by means of a gold ring which had resisted the corrosive effects of the lime into which he had thrown the body, not only the person murdered was to be identified but the locality of the crime and the man who committed it. So much was told to me before any of the book was written; and it will be recollected that the ring, taken by Drood to be given to his betrothed only if their engagement went on, was brought away with him from their last interview. Rosa was to marry Tartar, and Crisparkle the sister of Landless, who was himself, I think, to have perished in assisting Tartar finally to unmask and seize the murderer.

Nothing had been written, however, of the main parts of the design excepting what is found in the published numbers; there was no hint or preparation for the sequel in any notes of chapters in advance; and there remained not even what he had himself so sadly written of the book by Thackeray also interrupted by death. The evidence of matured designs never to be accomplished, intentions planned never to be executed, roads of thought marked out never to be traversed, goals shining in the distance never to be reached, was wanting here. It was all a blank.

Exhibit G

HOW WAS THE MURDER COMMITTED?
by
Edwin Charles

We can easily picture the scene. Edwin has returned from his walk down to the river with Landless after the Christmas Eve dinner-party; Jasper is waiting for him with two glasses of wine ready to drink "A Merry Christmas" to the new day which has now dawned. Edwin is a little melancholy. He is wondering how the "dear old fellow" (Jasper) will bear the news of his broken engagement when Grewgious tells him of it. He is wondering what that last curious look of Rosa's meant. He cannot shake off the eerie feeling aroused in him by the opium hag's mysterious words of "Ned" being a threatened person; but he drinks his wine (drugged, of course) with a cheery, "A Merry Christmas, dear old Jack," and sinks into a slumber from which he never awakens. The large black silk scarf, strongly and closely woven, is brought into requisition, and soon one of the spectres of the night becomes a gruesome fact, and Jasper sees his rival for the love of Rosa Bud a strangled corpse before him. Having possessed himself of the boy's watch and chain and shirt-pin (the only jewellery to his certain knowledge that he possesses) he proceeds to take the body to the tomb he has prepared for it. A difficult task, that, to carry the body downstairs and away to the churchyard in the Precincts. But not too difficult, for it *must* be done. After dark there is little fear of meeting anyone there "because of the awful hush that pervades that ancient pile, the cloisters, and the churchyard," and "because of the innate shrinking of dust with the breath of life in it from dust out of which the breath of life has passed" (Chapter XII). But on this Christmas night, when the boisterous gale has blown out many of the lamps (and the Precincts are never particularly well lighted), the chances of meeting anyone are almost nil. It may be that the gale helps him along with his awful burden; but, be that as it may, his fearful task is eventually finished, and to the howling of the wind, to the tossing and creaking of the trees, to the tearing and breaking of branches (fit accompaniment to so foul a deed) the body is placed in the tomb, and no trace of Edwin Drood revisits the light of the sun.

Exhibit H

THE DEMEANOUR OF MURDERERS
by
Charles Dickens

The recent trial of the greatest villain that ever stood in the Old Bailey dock, has produced the usual descriptions inseparable from such occasions. The public has read from day to day of the murderer's complete self-possession, of his constant coolness, of his profound composure, of his perfect equanimity. Some describers have gone so far as to represent him, occasionally rather amused than otherwise by the proceedings; and all the accounts that we have seen, concur in more or less suggesting that there is something admirable, and difficult to reconcile with guilt, in the bearing so elaborately set forth.

As whatever tends, however undesignedly, to insinuate this uneasy sense of incongruity into any mind, and to invest so abhorrent a ruffian with the slightest tinge of heroism, must be prejudicial to the general welfare, we revive the detestable subject with the hope of showing that there is nothing at all singular in such a deportment, but that it is always to be looked for and counted on, in the case of a very wicked murderer. The blacker the guilt, the stronger the probability of its being thus carried off.

In passing, we will express an opinion that Nature never writes a bad hand. Her writing, as it may be read in the human countenance, is invariably legible, if we come at all trained to the reading of it. Some little weighing and comparing are necessary. It is not enough in turning our eyes on the demon in the Dock, to say he has a fresh colour, or a high head, or a bluff manner, or what not, and therefore he does not look like a murderer, and we are surprised and shaken. The physiognomy and conformation of the Poisoner whose trial occasions these remarks, were exactly in accordance with his deeds; and every guilty consciousness he had gone on storing up in his mind, had set its mark upon him.

We proceed, within as short a compass as possible, to illustrate the position we have placed before our readers in the first paragraph of this paper.

The Poisoner's demeanour was considered exceedingly remarkable, because of his composure under trial, and because of the confident expectation of acquittal which he professed to the last, and under the influence of which he, at various times during his incarceration, referred to the plans he entertained for the future when he should be free again.

Can any one, reflecting on the matter for five minutes, suppose it possible—we do not say probable, but possible—that in the breast of this Poisoner there were surviving, in the days of his trial, any lingering traces of sensibility, or any wrecked fragment of the quality which we call sentiment? Can the profoundest or the simplest man alive, believe that in such a heart there could have been left, by that time, any touch of Pity? An objection to die, and a special objection to be killed, no doubt he had; and with that objection very strong within him for divers very weighty reasons, he was—*not* quite composed. Distinctly *not* quite composed, but, on the contrary, very restless. At one time, he was incessantly pulling on and pulling off his glove; at another time, his hand was constantly passing over and over his face; and the thing most instanced in proof of his composure, the perpetual writing and scattering about of little notes, which, as the verdict drew nearer and nearer, thickened from a sprinkling to a heavy shower, is in itself a proof of miserable restlessness. Beyond this emotion, which any lower animal would have, with an apprehension on it of a similar fate, what was to be expected from such a creature but insensibility? I poison my friend in his drink, and I poison my friend in his bed, and I poison my wife, and I poison her memory, and do you look to ME, at the end of such a career as mine, for sensibility? I have not the power of it even in my own behalf, I have lost the manner of it, I don't know what it means, I stand contemptuously wondering at you people here when I see you moved by this affair. In the Devil's name, man, have you heard the evidence of that chambermaid, whose tea I should like to have the sweetening of? Did you hear her describe the agonies in which my friend expired? Do you know that it was my trade to be learned in poisons, and that I foresaw all that, and considered all that, and knew, when I stood at his bedside looking down upon his face turned to me for help on its road to the grave through the frightful gate then swinging on its hinges, that in so many hours or minutes all those horrors would infallibly ensue? Have you heard that, after my poisonings, I have had to face the circumstances out, with friends and enemies, doctors, undertakers, all sorts of men, and have uniformly done it; and do you wonder that I face it out with you? Why not? What right or reason can you have to expect anything else of me? Wonder! You might wonder, indeed, if you saw me moved, here now before you. If I had any natural human feeling for my face to express, do you imagine that those medicines of my prescribing and administering would ever have been taken from my hand?

Why, man, my demeanour at this bar is the natural companion of my crimes, and, if it were a tittle different from what it is, you might even begin reasonably to doubt whether I had ever committed them!

The Poisoner had a confident expectation of acquittal. We doubt as little that he really had some considerable hope of it, as we do that he made a pretence of having more than he really had. Let us consider, first, if it be wonderful that he should have been rather sanguine. He had poisoned his victims according to his carefully laid plans; he had got them buried out of his way; he had murdered, and forged, and yet kept his place as a good fellow and a sporting character; he had made a capital friend of the coroner, and a serviceable traitor of the postmaster; he was a great public character, with a special Act of Parliament for his trial; the choice spirits of the Stock Exchange were offering long odds in his favour, and, to wind up all, here was a tip-top Counsellor bursting into tears for him, saying to the jury, three times over, 'You dare not, you dare not, you dare not!' and bolting clean out of the course to declare his belief that he was innocent. With all this to encourage him, with his own Derby-day division of mankind into knaves and fools, and with his own secret knowledge of the difficulties and mysteries with which the proof of Poison had been, in the manner of the Poisoning, surrounded, it would have been strange indeed if he were not borne up by some idea of escape. But, why should he have professed himself to have more hope of escape than he really entertained? The answer is, because it belongs to that extremity, that the villain in it should not only declare a strong expectation of acquittal himself, but should try to infect all the people about him with it. Besides having an artful fancy (not wholly without foundation) that he disseminates by that means an impression that he is innocent; to surround himself in his narrowed world with this fiction is, for the time being, to fill the jail with a faintly rose-coloured atmosphere, and to remove the gallows to a more agreeable distance. Hence, plans are laid for the future, communicated with an engaging candour to turnkeys, and discussed in a reliant spirit. Even sick men and women, over whom natural death is impending, constantly talk with those about them on precisely the same principle.

It may be objected that there is some slight ingenuity in our endeavours to resolve the demeanour of this Poisoner into the same features as the demeanour of every other very wicked and very hardened criminal in the same strait, but that a parallel would be better than argument. We have no difficulty in finding a parallel; we have no difficulty in finding scores, beyond the almost insuperable difficulty of finding, in the criminal records, as deeply-dyed a murderer. To embarrass these remarks, however, with references to cases that have passed out of the general memory, or have never been widely known, would be to render the discussion very irksome. We will confine ourselves to a famous instance. We will not even ask if it be so long ago since Rush was tried, that *his* demeanour is forgotten. We will call Thurtell into court, as one of the murderers best remembered in England.

With the difference that the circumstances of Thurtell's guilt are not comparable in atrocity with those of the Poisoner's, there are points of strong resemblance between the two men. Each was born in a fair station, and educated in conformity with it; each murdered a man with whom he had been on terms of intimate association, and for whom he professed a friendship at the time of the murder; both were members of that vermin-race of outer betters and blacklegs, of whom some worthy samples were presented on both trials, and of whom, as a community, mankind would be blessedly rid, if they could all be, once and for ever, knocked on the head at a blow. Thurtell's demeanour was exactly that of the

Poisoner's. We have referred to the newspapers of his time, in aid of our previous knowledge of the case; and they present a complete confirmation of the simple fact for which we contend. From day to day, during his imprisonment before his trial, he is described as 'collected and resolute in his demeanour,' as 'rather mild and conciliatory in his address,' as being visited by 'friends whom he receives with cheerfulness,' as 'remaining firm and unmoved,' as 'increasing in confidence as the day which is to decide his fate draws nigh,' as 'speaking of the favourable result of the trial with his usual confidence.' On his trial, he looks 'particularly well and healthy.' His attention and composure are considered as wonderful as the Poisoner's; he writes notes as the Poisoner did; he watches the case with the same cool eye; he 'retains that firmness for which, from the moment of his apprehension, he has been distinguished'; he 'carefully assorts his papers on a desk near him'; he is (in this being singular) his own orator, and makes a speech in the manner of Edmund Kean, on the whole not very unlike that of the leading counsel for the Poisoner, concluding, as to his own innocence, with a So help me God! Before his trial, the Poisoner says he will be at the coming race for the Derby. Before his trial, Thurtell says, 'that after his acquittal he will visit his father, and will propose to him to advance the portion which he intended for him, upon which he will reside abroad.' (So Mr. Manning observed, under similar circumstances, that when all that nonsense was over, and the thing wound up, he had an idea of establishing himself in the West Indies.) When the Poisoner's trial is yet to last another day or so, he enjoys his half-pound of steak and his tea, wishes his best friends may sleep as he does, and fears the grave 'no more than his bed.' (See the Evening Hymn for a Young Child.) When Thurtell's trial is yet to last another day or so, he takes his cold meat, tea, and coffee, and 'enjoys himself with great comfort'; also, on the morning of his execution, he wakes from as innocent a slumber as the Poisoner's, declaring that he has had an excellent night, and that he hasn't dreamed 'about this business.' Whether the parallel will hold to the last, as to 'feeling very well and comfortable,' as to 'the firm step and perfect calmness,' as to 'the manliness and correctness of his general conduct,' as to 'the countenance unchanged by the awfulness of the situation'—not to say as to bowing to a friend, from the scaffold 'in a friendly but dignified manner'—our readers will know for themselves when we know too.

It is surely time that people who are not in the habit of dissecting such appearances, but who are in the habit of reading about them, should be helped to the knowledge that, in the worst examples they are the most to be expected, and the least to be wondered at. That, there is no inconsistency in them, and no fortitude in them. That, there is nothing in them but cruelty and insensibility. That, they are seen, because the man is of a piece with his misdeeds; and that it is not likely that he ever could have committed the crimes for which he is to suffer, if he had not this demeanour to present, in standing publicly to answer for them.

Notes

Prefatory Quote

1. K. J. Fielding, *Charles Dickens: A Critical Introduction* (New York: David McKay Co., 1958), page 197.

Chapter II. Latecomers

1. This dubious claim has been accepted even by some who think that Datchery is a new character. For instance, see S. C. Roberts's introduction to *The Mystery of Edwin Drood* (London: Oxford University Press, 1956), pages x–xi.
2. Ibid., pages 1, 206, 278.

Chapter IV. Bucket and Datchery

1. As noted in my second chapter, Bucket was introduced in *Bleak House* when 35 percent of that novel had been completed; Datchery arrived when approximately 37 percent of the projected total of *Edwin Drood* had been written.
2. Because Mr. Bucket is a thoroughly masculine character, "making a leg" must be a man's gesture, not a woman's, and as such all but eliminates the possibility that Helena Landless is Dick Datchery.

Chapter V. Datchery Discovered

1. Sir David Wilkie, *The Wilkie Gallery* (London: J. S. Virtue & Co., 1848–1850), facing page 40. For a photograph of Wilkie's original painting, see Hans Karlinger, *München und die Kunst des 19. Jahrhunderts* (Munich: Lama-Verlag, 1966), page 195, plate 75.
2. Allan Cunningham, *The Life of Sir David Wilkie* (London: John Murray, 1843), Vol. II, page 24.
3. I can't insist upon the wig because five Dickens characters besides Dick Datchery share the same combination of white or gray hair and black

eyebrows, and none of them appears to be wearing a wig: Mr. Wickfield in *David Copperfield* (Chapter 15); Matthew Pocket in *Great Expectations* (Chapter 23); Brooker in *Nicholas Nickleby* (Chapter 44); Dr. Manette in *A Tale of Two Cities* (Book I, Chapter 6); and Jack Governor in the short story "The Haunted House."

4. Jack Lindsay maintains that Datchery owes his surname to smuggler Miles Datchet of Lady Rosina Bulwer-Lytton's novel *Cheveley* (1839), a vitriolic attack on her estranged husband, Dickens's friend and fellow novelist Edward Bulwer-Lytton (Jack Lindsay, *Charles Dickens* [London: Andrew Dakers Ltd., 1950], page 408). Yet it's not likely that when Dickens started *Edwin Drood,* thirty years after *Cheveley's* publication, he would have remembered a minor character like Datchet, and even less likely that he would have dredged up a reminder of his friend's disastrous marriage—for Bulwer-Lytton was still alive in 1870.
5. Percy T. Carden, *The Murder of Edwin Drood* (New York: G. P. Putnam's Sons, 1920), page 120. Reprinted in this volume as Exhibit D.
6. For the establishment of the Detective Department and some incidents from Stephen Thornton's career, see Belton Cobb, *The First Detectives* and *Critical Years at the Yard* (London: Faber & Faber Ltd., 1957 and 1956 respectively).

Chapter VI. Relevant Crimes

1. George A. Sala, *Things I Have Seen and People I Have Known* (London: Cassell & Co., 1894), Vol. I, pages 76 and 95.
2. Philip Collins, *Dickens and Crime* (Bloomington: Indiana University Press, 1968), page 253.
3. Charles Dickens, *The Uncommercial Traveller,* Chapter VII, "Travelling Abroad."
4. Ibid., Chapter XIX, "Some Recollections of Mortality."
5. Charles Dickens, "The Demeanour of Murderers," *Household Words,* June 14, 1856, reprinted in *Miscellaneous Papers.* See Exhibit H.
6. Ibid. Howard Duffield calls John Jasper an Indian Thug and Felix Aylmer gives him an Egyptian mother, but in my book he's just another homegrown English murderer like Thurtell, Wainewright, Manning, and Palmer.
7. Quoted from *The Somerset and Wilts Journal,* July 7, 1860, by John Rhode (Cecil Street), *The Case of Constance Kent* (London: Geoffrey Bles, 1928), page 83.

8. Arthur Griffiths, *Mysteries of Police and Crime* (London: Cassell & Co., 1898), Vol. I, page 26.
9. Quoted by Cobb, *Critical Years,* page 59. This work is my primary source for details of the Emsley case, including some of the quotations by its participants.
10. Sometimes miscalled James Mullins (his son's name).
11. *Annual Register* (London: Longmans, Green, et al., 1860), page 543.
12. Kate Dickens Perugini, "Edwin Drood and the Last Days of Charles Dickens," *Pall Mall Magazine,* June 1906. Reprinted in W. Robertson Nicoll's *The Problem of 'Edwin Drood'* (London: Hodder & Stoughton, 1912), pages 28–43.
13. William R. Hughes, *A Week's Tramp in Dickens-Land* (London: Chapman & Hall, 1893), pages 115–116.
14. Timothy Cavanagh, *Scotland Yard Past and Present* (London: Chatto & Windus, 1893), page 85; and George Dilnot, *Scotland Yard, Its History and Organization* (London: Geoffrey Bles, 1929), page 233.
15. Cavanagh, op. cit., page 67.
16. Griffiths, op. cit., page 81.

Chapter VII. A Dangerous Voyage

1. I prefer accounts sympathetic to Popay, such as those in Cobb, *First Detectives,* pages 91–92; and Douglas G. Browne, *The Rise of Scotland Yard* (New York: G. P. Putnam's Sons, 1956), pages 104–106.
2. Cobb, *First Detectives,* page 92.
3. Cavanagh, op. cit., page 85.
4. Ibid., page 87.
5. Information kindly furnished by Mr. J. B. Devlin, Black Museum, New Scotland Yard.
6. Carden, loc. cit. See Exhibit D.
7. Placing Jasper's confrontation with the protagonists on the anniversary of Drood's disappearance was first suggested by Richard A. Proctor in his *Watched by the Dead* (London: W. H. Allen, 1887), pages 52 and 135.
8. Richard M. Baker, *The Drood Murder Case* (Berkeley: University of California Press, 1951), page 142. The quotation (or paraphrase) is from *Drood,* Chapter 16.

Chapter VIII. Artistically Tenable

1. Montagu Saunders, *The Mystery in the Drood Family* (Cambridge: Cambridge University Press, 1914), page 82.
2. Charles Dickens, "The Signal-Man," from *Mugby Junction,* the Christmas 1866 number of *All the Year Round.*
3. Information furnished by Mr. J. B. Devlin, Black Museum, New Scotland Yard.
4. Cobb, *First Detectives,* pages 153–154.
5. Proctor, op. cit., page 159.
6. Nicoll, op. cit., pages 82–89.
7. John Forster, *The Life of Charles Dickens* (London: Chapman & Hall, 1874), Vol. III, pages 429–432.
8. Aubrey Boyd, "A New Angle on the Drood Mystery," *Washington University Studies, Humanistic Series,* October 1921, pages 51–53.
9. Browne, op. cit., page 123.
10. Listed in *A Treasury of Victorian Detective Stories,* Everett F. Bleiler, editor (New York: Charles Scribner's Sons, 1979), pages 4 and 71.
11. None of the detectives from the novels cited, not even Cuff, was the leading character of the story in which he appeared. Like most other detectives in novels published before 1870, they were supporting players who made their entrance, contributed their moiety to the solution of the mystery, and then retired into the wings. For this reason, R. F. Stewart calls them collectively "the guest detectives"—a fraternity that almost surely includes Dick Datchery. After putting Jasper behind bars, Datchery too was probably destined to fade quietly into the background. See R. F. Stewart, *And Always a Detective* (Newton Abbot: David & Charles, 1980), page 177.
12. See "*The Mystery of Edwin Drood.* Suggestions for a Conclusion" (published anonymously, but attributed by *The Wellesley Index* to H. S. Edwards), *Cornhill Magazine,* Vol. 49 (March 1884), pages 308–317. Also see letters from "H. E." (Edwards again?) and "J. B." defending the detective theory against the attacks of Thomas Foster (Richard Proctor) in *Knowledge Magazine,* Vol. 5 (June 27, 1884), pages 478–479; Vol. 6 (September 12, 1884), pages 209–210; Vol. 6 (December 5, 1884), pages 471–472; and Vol. 7 (January 2, 1885), pages 16–17.

Chapter IX. The Professional Touch

1. Don Richard Cox, "Shaw on *Edwin Drood*: Some Unpublished Letters," *The Dickensian,* Vol. 84, No. 414 (Spring 1988), page 29.

Chapter X. Surprise Endings

1. Of 65 solutions to *The Mystery* tallied by Philip Hobsbaum, 40 (62 percent) held that Jasper murdered Drood, 2 (3 percent) that someone else killed him, and 23 (35 percent) that Drood survived. (Percentages added.) Philip Hobsbaum, *A Reader's Guide to Charles Dickens* (New York: Farrar, Straus & Giroux, 1972), page 276.
2. Felix Aylmer, *The Drood Case* (New York: Barnes & Noble, 1964), page 98.
3. Lillian De La Torre, "John Dickson Carr's Solution to *The Mystery of Edwin Drood,*" *The Armchair Detective,* Vol. 14, No. 4 (1981), pages 291–294.
4. Arthur J. Cox, "Dickens' Last Book: More Mysteries Than One," *The Armchair Detective,* Vol. 14, No. 1 (1981), pages 31–35.
5. Aylmer, op. cit., pages 29–30.
6. Great mysteries as a rule are not unduly difficult for readers to solve—witness *The Moonstone, The Hound of the Baskervilles,* and *The Maltese Falcon.* The magic lies elsewhere.
7. In such articles as "Pet Prisoners," "The Demeanour of Murderers," "The Murdered Person," "Murderous Extremes," and "Five New Points of Criminal Law," all of which are available in most editions of *Miscellaneous Papers.*
8. Philip Collins, op. cit., page 254.
9. Norman Donaldson, in his introduction to *Lady Audley's Secret* by Mary Elizabeth Braddon (New York: Dover Publications Inc., 1974), pages v and x.
10. Ibid., page vii.
11. Walter Dexter, editor, *The Letters of Charles Dickens,* Volume III, (Bloomsbury: Nonesuch Press, 1938), pages 678, 699, and 700.

Chapter XI. Proof of Death

1. Gavin Brend, himself a Resurrectionist, first employed the word in this sense in his article "*Edwin Drood* and the Four Witnesses," *The Dickensian,* Vol. 52, No. 317 (December 1955), page 20. "Undertakers" is Brend's label for those of us who believe Edwin is dead.
2. See Dickens's letter, dated 2 September 1869, to Robert Lytton (Baker, op. cit., page 106). The page of notes on which the tentative titles appear bears the date 20 August 1869, just thirteen days earlier.
3. Nicoll, op. cit., pages 42–43.
4. Augustin Daly, "The 'Mystery' Solved," in *Bill of the Play for the Fifth Avenue Theatre,* September 5, 1871, page 3 (reprinted here as Exhibit E). The original playbill is in the uncatalogued theatrical programs collection of the Folger Shakespeare Library, Washington, D.C., and a copy on microfilm is available for loan from the University of Illinois, Champaign-Urbana–see Augustin Daly, *Archives,* in *The National Union Catalog Pre-1956 Imprints,* Vol. 131, page 682, entry ND 0018725.
5. Ibid.
6. Ibid.
7. Ibid. The fact that Augustin Daly printed Collins's letter "without abridgement" is important, because to date I have not been able to track down any of the original letters to the playwright from Dickens Junior, Fildes, and Collins. Nevertheless, there is reason to hope they still exist. Would anyone out there who knows what became of these letters please contact me through my publisher?
8. Joseph Francis Daly, *The Life of Augustin Daly* (New York: Macmillan, 1917), pages 107–108. Joseph Daly made a few minor editorial revisions to Collins's letter, the most noticeable of which occurs in the first sentence of the third paragraph, which reads in the playbill, "As to anything further it must be purely conjectional." The wording in the biography is, "As to any theory further it must be purely conjectural."
9. Forster, op. cit., pages 425–426.
10. Strangely enough, considering that Charles Collins's letter has been reprinted in *The Life of Augustin Daly* (1917), *The Dickensian* (1919 and 1955), Felix Aylmer's *Drood Case* (1964), and the Clarendon edition of *Edwin Drood* (1972), it has been overlooked by such writers as Stephen Leacock (1936), Richard Baker (1951), Edgar Johnson (1952), Sylvère Monod (1968), Audrey Peterson (1984), and Wendy Jacobson (1986), to name just a few.

11. Joseph Hatton, *People,* November 19, 1905. Quoted by Nicoll, op. cit., pages 43–44.
12. Hughes, op. cit., page 140.
13. Charles Dickens, *A Tale of Two Cities and The Mystery of Edwin Drood,* with introductions to both novels by Charles Dickens the Younger (New York and London: Macmillan & Co.), page 333. The title page gives the year of publication as 1896, but on the page following is the entry "Copyright, 1895, By MACMILLAN AND CO." Macmillan later reissued *The Mystery of Edwin Drood* (without *A Tale of Two Cities*) in editions published in 1923, 1925, and 1931, but the introduction contained in these later editions is merely a reprint of the one copyrighted in 1895, Charles Dickens the Younger having died in 1896.
14. Augustin Daly, loc. cit.
15. Alice Meynell, "How Edwin Drood Was Illustrated," *Century* magazine, February 1884, pages 522–528. Twenty years later, in a letter to G. F. Gadd dated May 2, 1904, Fildes denied that he had ever actually drawn Jasper wearing the scarf. See W. Laurence Gadd, "Sir Luke Fildes and *Edwin Drood,*" *Dickensian*, Vol. 23, No. 203 (Summer 1927), pages 159–160.
16. Hughes, op. cit., page 140.
17. Aylmer, op. cit., page 207.
18. Nicoll, op. cit., page 55.
19. L. V. Fildes, *Luke Fildes, R.A.; A Victorian Painter* (London: Michael Joseph, 1968), page 17.
20. Nicoll, op. cit., pages 32–36.
21. Sir Arthur Helps, *Correspondence of Sir Arthur Helps KCB,* edited by E. A. Helps (London: John Lane, 1917), pages 280–281.
22. Proctor, op. cit., page 151.
23. It's *the author himself* who kills off the victims in his stories. Charles Dickens killed Paul Dombey (and cried when he did it); he killed Nancy of *Oliver Twist* (over and over again in his public readings); he killed Little Nell and Tigg Montague and Mr. Tulkinghorn and all the rest. And he confessed repeatedly that he had killed Edwin Drood: twice in his own handwriting, in his notes for the novel; and orally to Charles Collins, to John Forster, and to his son Charles. To Luke Fildes, he all but confessed. Felix Aylmer contends that John Forster's outline of the story, being hearsay evidence, would be excluded in a court of law (op. cit., page 3). Mr. Aylmer is wrong. Hearsay or not, the confession of the accused person *is* admissible in English criminal law. For

the rules of evidence, see Sir Harold Richard Scott, editor, *The Concise Encyclopedia of Crime and Criminals* (New York: Hawthorn Books Inc., 1961), pages 139–140.

Chapter XII. Almost Perfect

1. Fildes opts for strangulation in the accounts given to Alice Meynell and William R. Hughes (cited above in Chapter XI), as does Dickens the Younger in the play he wrote in collaboration with Joseph Hatton (Nicoll, op. cit., page 48).
2. Baker, op. cit., pages 133–137.
3. Edwin Charles provides an exceptionally well-written account of this method of murder, reprinted here as Exhibit G. Edwin Charles, *Keys to the Drood Mystery* (London: Collier, 1908), pages 58–61.
4. Carden, op. cit., pages 37–38, 123–124.

Chapter XIII. The First Confrontation

1. There's also a legal principle involved here. Lord Hale stated it succinctly: "I never will allow a person to be convicted of murder before me, unless I have the direct testimony of some person who saw the fatal blow struck, or unless the body of the murdered person be found." As there was no eyewitness to Jasper's crime, he could have been convicted of murder (as Forster and Fildes imply he was) only if the prosecution produced enough of Drood's body to prove that the remains alleged to be his were human. Forensic medicine being in its infancy when Dickens wrote, it would have been impossible to establish anyone's death based upon the pile of dust and ashes to which some writers reduce poor Edwin's corpse, even with the fateful ring in it. Knowing this, Dickens would have provided the coroner with (at least) a skeleton to identify as Drood's.
2. Charles Dickens and Leon Garfield (continuator), *The Mystery of Edwin Drood* (New York: Pantheon Books, 1980), pages 292, 308.
3. Proctor, op. cit., page 74.
4. Andrew Lang, *The Puzzle of Dickens's Last Plot* (London: Chapman & Hall, 1905), pages 96–97.
5. Carden, op. cit., page 16.

6. Wilkie Collins's *Hide and Seek* (1854), a novel Dickens warmly praised, includes a step-by-step description of the methods used by its hero to obtain a duplicate key (New York: Dover Publications, 1981), pages 243–259. Perhaps Dickens remembered the process when John Jasper needed to copy the key to the Sapsea tomb.
7. For instance, the Opium Woman is Richard Baker's choice in *The Drood Murder Case,* page 89.
8. See Dickens's "Hunted Down," available in *The Mystery of Edwin Drood and Other Stories* (Boston: Houghton Mifflin, 1877), pages 405–430.
9. Baker, op. cit., page 162.
10. Presumably Charles Collins omitted any mention of the bottom-center vignette in his May 1871 letter to Augustin Daly because Dickens told him nothing more about it. Augustin Daly, loc. cit.
11. Lang, op. cit., page 85.
12. The preliminary sketch was first published in *The Dickensian,* Vol. 25, No. 211, pages 166–167. This issue was dated Summer 1929—after Proctor, Walters, Lang, Charles, Nicoll, Saunders, and Carden had published their books on *Edwin Drood.*
13. Augustin Daly, loc. cit.
14. S. M. Ellis, "Edwin Drood," *The Dickensian,* Vol. 25, No. 212 (Autumn 1929), page 323.
15. Augustin Daly, loc. cit.
16. Ibid.
17. Before the prisoner can be tried, the coroner must conduct an inquest to determine the cause of Edwin's death; the coroner's jury must return a verdict of willful murder; and the grand jury must indict John Jasper for the crime. But I expect Dickens would have made short work of these preliminaries.

Chapter XIV. John Jasper's Defense

1. Cyril Pearce Harvey, *The Advocate's Devil* (London: Stevens & Sons Ltd., 1958), pages 25–26.
2. Charles, op. cit., page 142.
3. A sergeant named James Otway got on Commissioner Mayne's black list by tricking an acquitted murderer into confessing to a lesser crime. So disapproving was Mayne of Otway's shabby trick that the sergeant,

who had shown some talent for detective work, was passed over when the Detective Department was formed. Cobb, *First Detectives,* pages 155–159.

4. For a glimpse of Jasper at his trial, see Dickens's description of John Thurtell's behavior in "The Demeanour of Murderers" (reprinted in this volume as Exhibit H). It's my belief that Dickens's perception of Thurtell's character strongly influenced his portrayal of John Jasper.
5. The crime of conspiracy in English law was first formulated to counter just such false accusations as Jasper claims are being made against him. See James Wallace Bryan, *The Development of the English Law of Conspiracy* (Baltimore: Johns Hopkins Press, 1909; reprinted by Da Capo Press, New York, 1970); and Percy Henry Winfield, *History of Conspiracy and Abuse of Procedures* (Cambridge: Cambridge University Press, 1921).
6. Proctor, op. cit., page 136. Proctor neglects to mention *how* Jasper kills Neville.
7. The first major scandal to involve Scotland Yard—the notorious Turf Frauds—did not occur until 1876, six years after Dickens died.
8. Perhaps the police would find the locksmith at the last possible moment, just as they found some silver plate stolen from Lord William Russell's home in time to introduce it into evidence against François Courvoisier on the last day of his trial. See Yseult Bridges, *Two Studies in Crime* (Hutchison of London, 1959), pages 85–87.

Chapter XV. The Second Confrontation

1. Philip Collins, op. cit., page 246.
2. Boyd, op. cit., page 77.
3. Baker, op. cit., pages 11 and 193.
4. Carden, op. cit., pages 107–111. Carden does not explain how Helena got the key to the Drood sarcophagus.
5. Baker, op. cit., page 89.
6. Forster, op. cit., pages 425–426.
7. There are two versions of the portrait painter's story. The earlier, untitled, shorter version appears as the first of "Four Ghost Stories"; it was originally published in *All the Year Round* on September 14, 1861. The second, longer version, actually bearing the title "The Portrait

Painter's Story," appeared in *AYR* on October 5, 1861, and was (according to Dickens) written by the artist himself. "The Trial for Murder," published in the Christmas number of *AYR* for 1865, was the sixth of "Doctor Marigold's Prescriptions."

8. In Dion Boucicault's play *The Corsican Brothers* (1852), one of the greatest hits of the nineteenth-century theatre, a murdered man's ghost reveals to his twin brother in a vision how and by whom he was killed. Dickens planned to take this concept a step further by having the slain twin show his survivor (perhaps in a dream) how to force his killer to confess.
9. Forster, loc. cit.
10. Boyd, op. cit., page 51.
11. Saunders, op. cit., page 7.
12. Rosina Lytton Bulwer, *Cheveley; or, The Man of Honour* (Paris: Baudry's European Library, 1839), pages 363 ff. Rosina, the estranged wife of Lord Lytton, preferred "Lytton Bulwer" to "Bulwer-Lytton."
13. By an eerie coincidence that Dickens himself would have appreciated, Mary Elizabeth Braddon confronted a murderer with a fake ghost in her short story "Levison's Victim," published within a month or two of Dickens's death. See *Belgravia* magazine, Volume 10 (1870), page 329.
14. In a letter to W. H. Wills dated June 30, 1867. Quoted by Baker, op. cit., page 17.
15. Forster, loc. cit.
16. "Je suis Vidocq!" and "I am Hawkshaw, the detective!" still reverberate after more than a century, and Datchery's cry, "I am Sergeant Thatcher of Scotland Yard!" has something of the same ring to it. But imagine the buffer whipping off his wig and exclaiming, "I am Helena Landless!" Could Dickens really have contemplated such an absurdity? And making Datchery shallow Edwin, gloomy Bazzard, or angular Grewgious isn't much of an improvement.

Chapter XVII. The Wicked Man

1. Nicoll, op. cit., pages 31–32.
2. Saunders, loc. cit.

3. For an eyewitness report of Thurtell's trial, see Anonymous, *The Fatal Effects of Gambling exemplified in the Murder of William Weare* (London: Thomas Kelly, 1824). For a more recent account, try *Trial of Thurtell and Hunt,* Eric R. Watson, editor (Edinburgh: William Hodge & Co., Ltd., 1920).
4. The Bible, King James Version, Ezekiel 18:27.
5. Baker, op. cit., page 73.
6. Except for overestimating the importance of the "Lost" placard, Baker provides an excellent, down-to-earth analysis of the Opium Woman's role in the novel. Ibid., pages 164–176.
7. Charles Forsyte, "The Sapsea Fragment—Fragment of What?," *The Dickensian,* Vol. 82, No. 408 (Spring 1986), pages 12–26. For more on dating the fragment, see Katharine M. Longley's "Letter to the Editor," *The Dickensian,* No. 409 (Summer 1986), pages 84–85.

Notes for Exhibits

A. "The Plot of 'Edwin Drood' " condenses pages 23–28 from Chapter II of John Cuming Walters's *Clues to Dickens's "Mystery of Edwin Drood"* (London: Chapman & Hall, 1905). I revised parts of three sentences—*printed in italics*—to remove some unwarranted inferences from Walters's synopsis.

B. "The Detective Police" was originally published in two installments (under the title "A Detective Police Party") in *Household Words* for July 27 and August 10, 1850. The two articles were combined and retitled when republished in *Reprinted Pieces.* The detective who boarded the emigrant ship *Victoria* looking for Mrs. Manning was Stephen Thornton.

C. "The Sofa" is the third of "Three 'Detective' Anecdotes" published in *Household Words* on September 14, 1850. Also republished in *Reprinted Pieces.*

D. "The Date of the Story" is Appendix II in Percy Carden's *The Murder of Edwin Drood,* pages 120–121.

E. "The 'Mystery' Solved" appears in *Bill of the Play for the Fifth Avenue Theatre,* Vol. I, No. 1 (September 5, 1871), page 3. The author of this brief article is not given in the playbill, but almost certainly it was written by the playwright-producer Augustin Daly himself. Incidentally, the play that night was Daly's *Divorce.* See Note 4, Chapter XI, for sources.

F. "Last Book" includes roughly the first three pages of Chapter II, Book Eleventh, from John Forster's *The Life of Charles Dickens.* Forster's footnotes have been omitted.

G. "How Was the Murder Committed?" reprints pages 58–61 from Chapter III of Edwin Charles's *Keys to the Drood Mystery.*

H. "The Demeanour of Murderers" first appeared in *Household Words* on June 14, 1856, and has been reprinted in *Miscellaneous Papers.* The unnamed Poisoner was William Palmer of Rugeley.

Select Bibliography

Dickens and Friends

Adrian, Arthur A. *Georgina Hogarth and the Dickens Circle.* London: Oxford University Press, 1957.

Cohen, Jane R. *Charles Dickens and his Original Illustrators.* Columbus: Ohio State University Press, 1980.

Collins, Philip. *Dickens and Crime.* Bloomington: Indiana University Press, 1968.

Davis, Earle. *The Flint and the Flame.* Columbia: University of Missouri Press, 1963.

Dexter, Walter, editor. *The Letters of Charles Dickens,* Vol. III. Bloomsbury: Nonesuch Press, 1938.

Dyson, A. E. *The Inimitable Dickens.* London: Macmillan, 1970.

Fielding, K. J. *Charles Dickens: A Critical Introduction.* New York: David McKay, 1958.

———. "The Dramatisation of *Edwin Drood.*" *Theatre Notebook,* Vol. 7 (1953), pages 52–58.

Forster, John. *The Life of Charles Dickens.* 3 vols., London: Chapman & Hall, 1872–1874.

Hobsbaum, Philip. *A Reader's Guide to Charles Dickens.* New York: Farrar, Strauss & Giroux, 1972.

Hughes, William R. *A Week's Tramp in Dickens-Land.* London: Chapman & Hall, 1893.

Leacock, Stephen. *Charles Dickens, His Life and Work.* Garden City, N.Y.: Doubleday Doran, 1936.

Lindsay, Jack. *Charles Dickens.* London: Andrew Dakers, 1950.

Mankowitz, Wolf. *Dickens of London.* New York: Macmillan, 1976.

Monod, Sylvère. *Dickens the Novelist.* Norman: University of Oklahoma Press, 1968.

Sala, George Augustus. *Charles Dickens.* London: George Routledge & Sons, 1870.

———. *Things I Have Seen and People I Have Known.* 2 vols., London: Cassells, 1894.
Storey, Gladys. *Dickens and Daughter.* London: Frederick Muller, 1939.
Symons, Julian. *Charles Dickens.* New York: Roy Publishers, 1951.

Edwin Drood

Aylmer, Felix. *The Drood Case.* New York: Barnes & Noble, 1964.
Baker, Richard M. *The Drood Murder Case.* Berkeley–Los Angeles: University of California Press, 1951.
Boyd, Aubrey. "A New Angle on the Drood Mystery." *Washington University Studies: Humanistic Series,* October 1921.
Carden, Percy T. *The Murder of Edwin Drood.* New York: G. P. Putnam's Sons, 1920.
Charles, Edwin. *Keys to the Drood Mystery.* London: Collier, 1908.
Daly, Augustin. "The 'Mystery' Solved." In *Bill of the Play for the Fifth Avenue Theatre,* September 5, 1871.
Dickens, Charles. *The Mystery of Edwin Drood.* Edited by Margaret Cardwell. Oxford: Clarendon Press, 1972.
———. Edited by Arthur J. Cox. Introduction by Angus Wilson. Harmondsworth: Penguin Books, 1974.
———. Completed by W. E. C. (Walter E. Crisp). London: J. M. Ouseley & Son, 1914.
———. Completed by Leon Garfield. New York: Pantheon Books, 1980.
———. Completed by Thomas Power James ("The Spirit-Pen"). Brattleboro, Vt.: T. P. James, 1873.
———. Introduction by S. C. Roberts. London: Oxford University Press, 1956.
———. Introduction by Edwin Percy Whipple. Boston: Houghton Mifflin, 1877.
———. *A Tale of Two Cities and The Mystery of Edwin Drood.* Introductions by Charles Dickens the Younger. New York and London: Macmillan, 1896.
Edwards, H. S. "*The Mystery of Edwin Drood.* Suggestions for a Conclusion." *Cornhill Magazine,* March 1884.
Forsyte, Charles. *The Decoding of Edwin Drood.* New York: Charles Scribner's Sons, 1980.
Graeme, Bruce. *Epilogue.* London: Hutchison & Co., 1933.
Harris, Edwin. *John Jasper's Gatehouse.* Rochester, England: Mackays Ltd., 1931.

Jackson, Henry. *About Edwin Drood.* Cambridge: Cambridge University Press, 1911.
Jacobson, Wendy S. *Companion to The Mystery of Edwin Drood.* London: Allen & Unwin, 1986.
Kerr, Orpheus C. (Robert Henry Newell). *The Cloven Foot.* New York: Carleton, 1870.
Lang, Andrew. *The Puzzle of Dickens's Last Plot.* London: Chapman & Hall, 1905.
Ley, J. W. T. *The Trial of John Jasper for the Murder of Edwin Drood.* London: Chapman & Hall, 1914.
Meynell, Alice. "How Edwin Drood Was Illustrated." *Century* magazine, February 1884.
Morford, Henry. *John Jasper's Secret.* Philadelphia: T. B. Peterson & Brothers, 1871.
Nicoll, W. Robertson. *The Problem of 'Edwin Drood.'* London: Hodder & Stoughton, 1912.
Proctor, Richard A. *Watched by the Dead.* London: W. H. Allen, 1887.
Saunders, Montagu. *The Mystery in the Drood Family.* 1914. Reprint. New York: Haskell House, 1974.
Vase, Gillan. *A Great Mystery Solved.* Edited by Shirley Byron Jevons. London: Sampson Low, Marston & Co., 1920.
Walters, John Cuming. *Clues to Dickens's "Mystery of Edwin Drood."* London: Chapman & Hall, 1905.
———. *The Complete Mystery of Edwin Drood.* Boston: Dana Estes, 1913.

Mystery Fiction

Bleiler, Everett F., editor. *A Treasury of Victorian Detective Stories.* New York: Charles Scribner's Sons, 1979.
Braddon, Mary Elizabeth (Maxwell). *Henry Dunbar.* London: Simpkin, Marshall, Hamilton, Kent & Co., no date. (First published 1864.)
———. *Lady Audley's Secret.* Introduction by Norman Donaldson. New York: Dover Publications, 1974 (1862).
———. "Levison's Victim." *Belgravia* magazine, Vol. 10 (1870), page 329.
Bulwer-Lytton, Edward. *Eugene Aram.* Boston: Little, Brown & Co., 1893 (1832).
———. *Paul Clifford.* London: George Routledge & Sons, 1877 (1830).
———. *Pelham; or, The Adventures of a Gentleman.* London: George Routledge & Sons, 1880 (1828).

Bulwer, Rosina Lytton. *Cheveley; or, The Man of Honour.* Paris: Baudry's European Library, 1839.
Collins, Wilkie. *Armadale.* 2 vols. St. Clair Shores, Mich.: Scholarly Press, 1976 (1866).
———. *Hide and Seek; or, The Mystery of Mary Grice.* New York: Dover Publications, 1981. (First published 1854, revised 1861.)
———. *Miss or Mrs.?* London: Chatto and Windus, 1925 (1871).
———. *The Moonstone.* New York: Pyramid Books, 1961 (1868).
———. *No Name.* New York: Stein & Day, 1966 (1862).
———. *The Queen of Hearts.* New York: Arno Press, 1976 (1859).
———. *Tales of Terror and the Supernatural.* Edited by Herbert van Thal. New York: Dover Publications, 1972.
———. *The Woman in White.* Harmondsworth: Penguin Books, 1974 (1860).
Cooper, James Fenimore. *The Ways of the Hour.* New York: Putnam, 1850.
Curtis, Robert. *Curiosities of Detection; or, The Sea-Coast Station, and Other Tales.* London: Ward & Lock, 1862.
———. *The Irish Police Officer.* London: Ward & Lock, 1861.
Dickens, Charles and Wilkie Collins. *No Thoroughfare.* New York: George Munro, 1884 (1867).
Dostoyevsky, Fyodor. *Crime and Punishment.* Translated by Constance Garnett. New York: Modern Library, 1950 (1866).
Felix, Charles. *The Notting Hill Mystery.* New York: Arno Press, 1976 (1865).
Godwin, William. *Things As They Are; or, The Adventures of Caleb Williams.* New York: Greenberg, 1926 (1794).
James, George Payne Raynsford. *Delaware; or, The Ruined Family.* London: George Routledge & Sons, 1880 (1833).
Le Fanu, Joseph Sheridan. *Uncle Silas: A Tale of Bartram-Haugh.* New York: Dover Publications, 1966 (1865).
———. *Wylder's Hand.* New York: Dover Publications, 1978 (1864).
Martel, Charles (Thomas Delf). *The Detective's Note-Book.* London: Ward & Lock, 1860.
———. *Diary of an Ex-Detective.* London: Ward & Lock, 1860.
Payn, James. *Found Dead,* London: Chapman & Hall, 1868.
———. *Lost Sir Massingberd.* London: Chatto & Windus, 1864.
Reach, Angus B. *Clement Lorimer; or, The Book with the Iron Clasps.* London: David Bogue, 1849.
Regester, Seeley (Metta Victoria Fuller Victor). *The Dead Letter.* Boston: Gregg Press, 1979 (1867).

Richmond, Thomas. *Richmond: Scenes in the Life of a Bow Street Runner.* Introduction by E. F. Bleiler. New York: Dover Publications, 1976 (1827).

Simms, William Gilmore. *Martin Faber, The Story of a Criminal, and Other Tales.* New York: Arno Press, 1976 (1837).

Speight, Thomas W. *Under Lock and Key.* New York: Arno Press, 1976 (1869).

Trollope, Thomas Adolphus. *A Siren.* New York: Arno Press, 1976 (1870).

Warren, Samuel. *Experiences of a Barrister and Confessions of an Attorney.* New York: Arno Press, 1976 (1859).

"Waters" (William Russell?). *Experiences of a French Detective Officer,* by "Theodore Duhamel." London: William Glaisher, 185–.

———. *Experiences of a Real Detective,* by "Inspector F." London: Ward & Lock, 1863.

———. *Recollections of a Detective Police Officer.* Includes "Second Series." Introduction by Eric Osborne. London: Covent Garden Press, 1972. (First published 1856 and 1859.)

Whyte-Melville, George John. *M. or N.* New York: Arno Press, 1976 (1869).

Wood, Mrs. Henry (Ellen Price Wood). *East Lynne.* New Brunswick, N.J.: Rutgers University Press, 1984 (1861).

———. *Mrs. Halliburton's Troubles.* London: Richard Bentley & Son, 1895 (1862).

Plays and Playwrights

Booth, Michael, editor. *English Plays of the Nineteenth Century.* Oxford: Clarendon Press, 1969. Contains Dion Boucicault's *Corsican Brothers* (1852) and Tom Taylor's *Ticket-of-Leave Man* (1863), both of which may have influenced Dickens when he wrote *Edwin Drood.*

Boucicault, Dion. *The Dolmen Boucicault.* Edited by David Krause. Chester Springs, Pa.: Dufour Editions, 1965.

———. *Plays by Dion Boucicault.* Edited by Peter Thomson. Cambridge: Cambridge University Press, 1984.

Daly, Augustin. *Man and Wife and Other Plays.* Edited by Catherine Sturtevant. Princeton, N.J.: Princeton University Press, 1942.

———. *Plays by Augustin Daly.* Edited by Don B. Wilmeth and Rosemary Cullen. Cambridge: Cambridge University Press, 1984.

Daly, Joseph Francis. *The Life of Augustin Daly.* New York: Macmillan, 1917.

Fawkes, Richard. *Dion Boucicault.* London: Quartet Books, 1979.

Lewis, Leopold. *Henry Irving and The Bells.* Edited by David Mayer. Manchester University Press, 1980. Lewis based *The Bells* on *Le Juif Polonais* (1868) by Erckmann-Chatrian, which Dickens may have seen in France.
Molin, Sven Eric, and Robin Goodefellowe. *Dion Boucicault, the Shaughraun.* 2 vols., Washington D.C.: Proscenium Press, 1979.

Law, Crime, and Police

Altick, Richard D. *Victorian Studies in Scarlet.* New York: W. W. Norton, 1970.
Anonymous. *The Fatal Effects of Gambling exemplified in the Murder of William Weare.* London: Thomas Kelly, 1824.
Anonymous. *A Complete History and Development of All the Extraordinary Circumstances and Events Connected with the Murder of Mr. Weare.* London: Jones & Co., 1824.
Ballantine, William. *Some Experiences of a Barrister's Life.* 2 vols., London: Richard Bentley & Son, 1882.
Blom-Cooper, Louis, editor. *The Law as Literature.* London: The Bodley Head, 1961.
Bridges, Yseult. *Two Studies in Crime.* London: Hutchison of London, 1959.
Browne, Douglas G. *The Rise of Scotland Yard.* New York: G. P. Putnam's Sons, 1956.
Bryan, James Wallace. *The Development of the English Law of Conspiracy.* 1909. Reprint. New York: Da Capo Press, 1970.
Canler, Louis. *Autobiography of a French Detective from 1818–1858.* 1862. Reprint. New York: Arno Press, 1976.
Cavanagh, Timothy. *Scotland Yard Past and Present.* London: Chatto & Windus, 1893.
Clarkson, Charles Tempest, and J. Hall Richardson. *Police!* London: The Leadenhall Press, 1889.
Cobb, Belton. *Critical Years at the Yard.* London: Faber & Faber, 1956.
———. *The First Detectives.* London: Faber & Faber, 1957.
Dilnot, George. *Scotland Yard, Its History and Organization.* Centenary Edition. London: Geoffrey Bles, 1929.
———. Introduction to *The Trial of Professor John White Webster.* London: Geoffrey Bles, 1928.
Egan, Pierce. *Pierce Egan's Account of the Trial of John Thurtell and Joseph Hunt.* London: Knight & Lacey, 1824.
———. *Recollections of John Thurtell.* London: Knight & Lacey, 1824.

Fitzgerald, Percy. *Chronicles of Bow Street Police-Office.* 2 vols., London: Chapman & Hall, 1888.

Griffiths, Arthur. *Mysteries of Police and Crime.* 2 vols., London: Cassell & Co., 1898.

Harvey, Cyril Pearce. *The Advocate's Devil.* London: Stevens & Sons, 1958.

Howe, Sir Ronald. *The Story of Scotland Yard.* New York: Horizon Press, 1965.

Jones, George Henry. *Account of the Murder of the Late Mr. William Weare.* London: Sherwood, Jones & Co., 1824.

Lansdowne, Andrew. *A Life's Reminiscences of Scotland Yard.* London: Leadenhall Press, 1890.

Lee, W. L. Melville. *A History of the Police in England.* 1901. Reprint. Montclair, N.J.: Patterson Smith, 1971.

Littlechild, John George. *Reminiscences of Chief-Inspector Littlechild.* London: Leadenhall Press, 1894.

Neale, Erskine. *Dark Deeds.* London: Ward & Lock, 18—.

Pelham, Camden. *The Chronicles of Crime; or, The New Newgate Calendar.* 2 vols. London: Thomas Tegg, 1841.

Prothero, Margaret. *The History of the Criminal Investigation Department at Scotland Yard from Earliest Times Until To-day.* London: Herbert Jenkins, 1931.

Rhode, John (Cecil Street). *The Case of Constance Kent.* London: Geoffrey Bles, 1928.

Roughead, William, editor. *Burke and Hare.* Edinburgh: William Hodge, 1921.

Scott, Sir Harold Richard, editor. *The Concise Encyclopedia of Crime and Criminals.* New York: Hawthorn Books, 1961.

Thomson, Sir Basil. *The Story of Scotland Yard.* New York: Literary Guild, 1936.

Vidocq, Eugene François. *Memoirs of Vidocq, Principal Agent of the French Police Until 1827.* 1828–1829. Reprint. New York: Arno Press, 1976.

Watson, Eric R., editor. *Trial of Thurtell and Hunt.* Edinburgh and London: William Hodge, 1920.

Winfield, Percy Henry. *History of Conspiracy and Abuse of Procedures.* Cambridge: Cambridge University Press, 1921.

Odds and Ends

Cunningham, Allan. *The Life of Sir David Wilkie.* 3 vols., London: John Murray, 1843.

Dickens, Charles, Wilkie Collins, and others. *The Wreck of the Golden Mary.* 1856. Reprint. New York: Library Publishers, 1956.

Epstein, Diana. *Buttons.* New York: Walker & Co., 1968.

Fildes, L. V. *Luke Fildes, R. A., A Victorian Painter.* London: Michael Joseph, 1968.

Ford, Grace Horney. *The Button Collector's History.* Springfield, Mass.: Pond-Ekberg, 1943.

Gaskell, Mrs. (Elizabeth). *Mary Barton.* London: Everyman's Library, 1967 (1848).

Ousby, Ian. *Bloodhounds of Heaven: The Detective from Godwin to Doyle.* Cambridge, Mass.: Harvard University Press, 1976.

Peterson, Audrey. *Victorian Masters of Mystery.* New York: Frederick Ungar, 1984.

Thomson, David Croal. *The Life and Work of Luke Fildes, R. A.* London: Art Annual, 1895.

Wilkie, Sir David. *The Wilkie Gallery.* London: J. S. Virtue, 1848–1850.

Wilson, Edmund. *The Wound and the Bow.* New York: Oxford University Press, 1947.

Periodicals

The Armchair Detective, 1968 on.

The Dickensian, 1905 on.

The Dickens Quarterly, 1984 on.

The Dickens Studies Newsletter, 1970–1983.

The Dickens Studies Annual, 1970 on.